WORKING
WITH WOOD

WORKING WITH WOOD

THE BASICS OF CRAFTSMANSHIP

PETER KORN

Drawings by the author

The Taunton Press

Cover photos: Susan Kahn

Taunton
BOOKS & VIDEOS

for fellow enthusiasts

© 1993 by Peter Korn

First printing: May 1993
Printed in the United States of America

A FINE WOODWORKING Book
FINE WOODWORKING® is a trademark of The Taunton Press, Inc.,
registered in the U.S. Patent and Trademark Office.

The Taunton Press, 63 South Main Street,
Box 5506, Newtown, CT 06470-5506

Library of Congress Cataloging-in-Publication Data

Korn, Peter, 1951-
        Working with wood : the basics of
        craftsmanship / Peter Korn.
                    p.   cm.
        Includes index.
        "A Fine Woodworking book" — T.p. verso.
        ISBN 1-56158-041-4
        1. Woodwork.   I. Title.
        TT180.K64   1993   92-45027
        784'.08 — dc20   CIP

To Sarah, my wife, for her gift of joy and love.

ACKNOWLEDGMENTS

The six years I spent as director of the woodworking program at Anderson Ranch Arts Center were a special opportunity for professional growth and for exploring new skills such as writing. For their encouragement, I thank the entire staff and board, particularly ex-director Brad Miller.

I would also like to express my heartfelt appreciation to Harv Mastalir, my sometime Basic Woodworking co-instructor, who has taught me a thing or two and who was kind enough to read and comment upon the manuscript of this book; to master finisher Bob Flexner, for keeping me straight on the subtleties of finishes; and to Hal Smyer for making photography enjoyable and for patience with the Indigo Girls.

I have greatly enjoyed working with the staff of The Taunton Press. Particular appreciation to John Kelsey for believing in this book, to Andy Schultz for guidance and to Peter Chapman for editing with care and integrity.

Finally, and gratefully, I acknowledge my parents, Peggy Liss and Stephen Korn, for their constant love and support.

CONTENTS

INTRODUCTION

This book evolved from the Basic Woodworking workshop I have given nearly every summer since 1981. Class participants range from absolute beginners to experienced woodworkers who are competent with machinery but still need to master the hand skills so essential to fine craftsmanship. Like the course, this book presents indispensable information on wood characteristics, joinery and tools, before going on to offer a series of projects that build upon one another sequentially. We begin by milling a piece of wood four-square and end with construction of a dovetailed wall cabinet that incorporates a drawer and a frame-and-panel door. These exercises have worked well for my students over the years. If you read this book and carefully work through the projects, you will establish a solid foundation in woodworking craftsmanship that will enable you to build beautiful furniture with confidence.

Although I have taught graduate and undergraduate furniture design in a university and have given courses in drawing and design to skilled furniture makers, basic woodworking continues to be my favorite teaching experience. The excitement with which beginners approach the most mundane skills revitalizes my own sense of wonder at the miracle of craftsmanship. We begin with nothing more tangible than intent and end with a sensitive, sometimes beautiful object that will be an intimate part of our daily life. What comes in between is craftsmanship.

To understand craftsmanship we must ask not only "What has been made?" and "How has this been made?" but also "Who made this and why?" Craftsmanship is a relationship between the maker and the process of creation. It is not simply a set of skills one acquires, like the ability to read or drive a car. More than anything, craftsmanship is a matter of attitude: why a person chooses to devote time to such a demanding endeavor and to make a certain object of a certain appearance, and how the person goes about it.

In this context, craftsmanship is first and foremost an expression of the human spirit. I choose to work as a craftsman because the process answers a need of my spirit; the object I make is the physical expression of the interaction between spirit and matter. How is this different than the work of the artist?

The artist is not concerned with the utility of the created object, the craftsman is. I care that a chair be comfortable, sturdy and durable, that it look inviting to sit in, that its presence in a room be neither overbearing nor withdrawn. This care is implicit in every step of making the chair—in drawing up the plans, choosing the wood, maintaining my tools, milling the rough lumber to size, cutting the joinery, planing, scraping, sanding and applying the finish.

Craftsmanship is both attitude and skills. This book offers a foundation in both. Individual character will determine the pace of your growth as a craftsman and the nature of your work. In return, the practice of craftsmanship will affect your character.

There is no one right way to do anything in woodworking. The right way is the way that works best for you, and what works best is a balance between the time something takes, the tools available, the pleasure you take in the process and the quality of result you are looking for. In my shop I prefer hand tools over machinery for joining and smoothing surfaces; I like the quiet, the control and the communication between my hand and the work. Time is not as important to me as it is in a commercial shop. My personal concerns are quality and joy.

The methods and explanations offered in this book are understandings I have arrived at through 20 years of practice. I offer them not as the truth, but as one truth, as a starting point on your own journey into craftsmanship. As you continue learning you may seek out teachers who will provide deeper insight into many areas of expertise, but you should always remember that the most valuable teacher you will encounter is yourself. Practice is the most essential component to mastering craftsmanship. Learn from your mistakes and successes, and, above all, learn from your hands.

WOOD

Wood is special for the same reason that it is quirky—it is a natural material that comes from trees. Wind, sun, shade, soil, site, rainfall and competition with neighbors are among the variables that make each tree unique in the color, density, grain pattern and working characteristics of the lumber it yields. As we fashion wood into furniture, every board reveals an individual personality in response to our tools. Skilled craftsmanship begins with an understanding of the characteristics imparted to wood by biology and the vagaries of tree growth.

PHYSICAL PROPERTIES

A tree is composed of long cells that run through its trunk, limbs and branches. Basically, these cells are made of cellulose, the same material from which household sponges are made, and bound together with an adhesive called lignin.

You might picture a piece of wood as a bundle of straws (cells) held together with glue (lignin). The fibrous straws are difficult to break across their length, but relatively easy to pry apart from each other. This is why wood splits along the grain much more readily than across the grain.

CROSS SECTION OF A TREE

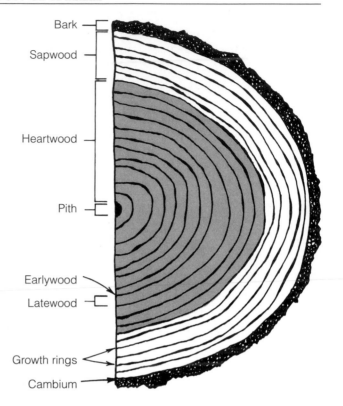

Bark

Sapwood

Heartwood

Pith

Earlywood

Latewood

Growth rings

Cambium

A cross section of a living tree shows the different types of growth. At the perimeter is the bark. The outer bark protects the tree from damage by insects, animals, the elements and abrasion. The inner bark carries nutrients created by photosynthesis in the leaves to a thin layer of living growth cells—the cambium.

All tree growth takes place in the cambium; cells toward its outside become new bark, cells toward its inside become new wood. Each year the cambium lays down a new outer ring of sapwood, and each year the interior ring of sapwood loses its ability to carry sap upwards and stiffens to become heartwood, the skeletal backbone of the tree. At the center of the tree is the pith.

When we think of walnut as a dark, richly colored wood, we are thinking of its heartwood. The sapwood of walnut, as of most species, is lighter in color and slightly softer. Some furniture makers use sapwood and heartwood; others prefer uniform color in their work and use only heartwood.

Trees in many climates grow more rapidly in spring than in summer. Within a single growth ring, this transition is revealed as changes in density and color. The interior of an annual ring, the "earlywood" laid down in spring, tends to be more porous and different in color than the "latewood" of summer growth.

WATER AND WOOD

Because the walls of wood cells are made of sponge-like material, they readily absorb moisture. Even a piece of "dry" wood, like the top of a dining table, gains and loses moisture as the humidity in the room changes with the weather and the season. The cell walls expand and contract with variations in moisture content, changing in width but staying virtually constant in length. When humidity increases, the tabletop expands across the grain but remains the same length.

The fact that wood fluctuates in dimension has required woodworkers throughout the centuries to come up with specialized techniques for permanently attaching one piece to another. These techniques are known collectively as "joinery" and are described in the next chapter.

A live tree felled for lumber contains two types of moisture, free moisture and bound moisture. Free moisture is the water that has been flowing through the cells; bound moisture is the water absorbed in their cellulose walls. In a live tree, the combined weight of free and bound moisture can exceed the weight of the wood itself. Lumber used for furniture making should be dried to the point where it contains no free water and bound moisture constitutes less than 10% by weight.

Removing all of the free water and most of the bound moisture isn't as simple as leaving a log out to dry, because wood shrinks as it dries, and uncontrolled shrinkage makes wood crack and split.

Imagine a freshly cut log lying on the ground. Moisture is evaporating through the bark and from the newly exposed ends. As the wood around the log's circumference dries it wants to shrink to a smaller diameter, but the interior hasn't lost much moisture yet and remains a constant size. As a result, the fibers of the shrinking exterior ring break apart, causing radial checks (splits) that extend inward from the surface. As moisture evaporates from the ends of the log, the ends want to shrink but are held in place by the wetter interior wood. What happens? The ends of the log split to relieve the tension.

A freshly cut log left to dry on its own is likely to yield lumber full of cracks. The solution is to cut a green log into planks and seal the plank ends with paint or wax so that all moisture has to evaporate through the sides. The planks should be "stickered"—stacked flat with spacers in between to allow air to circulate freely—and kept away from the sun or an extremely dry environment. This procedure is called "air-drying," and the rule of thumb is that it takes up to one year per inch of board thickness.

Commercial lumber companies can't afford to keep wood in inventory long enough for it to air-dry, so they use kilns to remove the moisture. Boards are stacked in the kiln with spacers in between. Warm, moist air is circulated through the kiln. The humidity of the air is reduced gradually to keep it just a step ahead of the drying wood. This controlled, gradual process, called "kiln-drying," prevents checking and splitting if done correctly.

EDGE GRAIN AND END GRAIN

To understand the meaning of edge grain and end grain, again picture a board as a bunch of straws held together with glue. At the four sides of the board, we are looking at the outside of the straws—this is called "edge grain" or "long grain." At either end of the board, we are looking at the open, round ends of the straws, the "end grain."

To reiterate an important point, end grain, being open, gains and loses moisture much more rapidly than edge grain. Unless the ends of a drying board are sealed, they shrink much faster than the rest of the board. Lumber that is going to be stored for any length of time should first have the ends sealed with wax, paint or finish to prevent end checks.

The difference between edge grain and end grain becomes significant when we glue wood together. The process of gluing two boards edge to edge can be looked at as re-assembling the straws in wood with man-made adhesive instead of lignin. Since modern glues are actually stronger than lignin, edge-grain joints are very reliable. End-grain glue joints, on the other hand, are very unreliable. The porous cells suck glue away from the contact point, and little bonding occurs. I have yet to see an end-grain glue joint I could not break apart with my bare hands.

CUTTING WITH THE GRAIN

Everyone has heard the expression "going against the grain." Its origin lies in the fact that the fibrous straws that make up wood split apart from one another more easily than they break across their length. If you've ever split logs with an ax you have probably noticed that the split follows the internal meanderings of the fibers rather than cutting straight down.

The blade of a hand plane, chisel or milling machine can be thought of as an ax. Once it enters the wood, the wood wants to split along its grain. If you are cutting with the grain, the wood splits back up toward the surface and no harm results. But if you are cutting against the grain, the wood wants to split down toward the core and "tearout" occurs.

CUTTING WITH AND AGAINST THE GRAIN

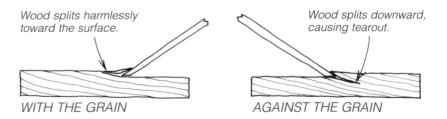

Wood splits harmlessly toward the surface.

Wood splits downward, causing tearout.

WITH THE GRAIN   AGAINST THE GRAIN

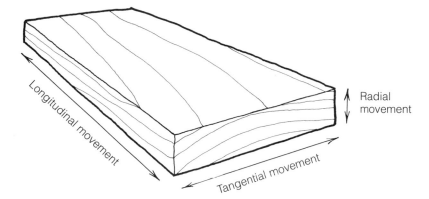

Wood expands as humidity increases and contracts as humidity decreases, but not equally in all directions. Tangential movement (more or less parallel to the growth rings) is greater than radial movement (perpendicular to the growth rings). Longitudinal movement (along the grain) is negligible.

RADIAL AND TANGENTIAL MOVEMENT

When wood shrinks or expands across the grain, it doesn't move at a uniform rate in all dimensions. Radial movement, which means movement perpendicular to the growth rings, is less than movement tangential to the growth rings. Although the difference is not dramatic, it is significant. A dowel will become oval as moisture content changes. A plainsawn board will cup, as explained below.

CUP, BOW AND TWIST

Wood warps in three ways: cupping, bowing and/or twisting. Cup is a curve across the width, bow is a curve along the length and twist is a spiral along the length.

In addition to changes in humidity, wood memory and internal stress are the major causes of wood movement. An example of memory occurs when a piece of wood is steambent into a curve. The crushed fibers on the inside of the curve want to regain their shape when they swell with humidity, much as a crumpled, dried-up sponge regains its flat, square shape when you drop it in dishwater. As the crushed fibers swell, they force the wood back toward its original straightness. Good bentwood furniture counters memory by structurally locking each curve in place.

Internal stress comes from the way a particular tree has grown or been dried. Sometimes, as you rip a board along its length on the table saw, the two free ends don't stay parallel to each other. They bend together to pinch the sawblade, or they spread apart. This movement can come from growth stress seeking a new equilibrium as material is removed from the board. It can also result from stress imparted by improper kiln-drying.

The radial checks in this fir post indicate that the tree grew in a spiral motion as it followed the daily movement of the sun.

Twist occurs because many trees grow with a slight spiral motion as they follow the sun in its daily orbit (see the photo above). A board that has been milled flat tends to recover some twist as changes in equilibrium occur through wood removal or fluctuations in moisture content.

Removing wood from the surface of a board can cause it to cup, bow or twist as the stress equilibrium is disturbed. Most of the time this is noticeable only if you are removing more than ⅛ in., but I once had the frustrating experience of trying to flatten an English brown oak tabletop that moved with every pass of my hand plane. Finally I had to shrug my shoulders and settle for something less than perfection. Such is the nature of woodworking.

If one side of a board is wetted, swelling will cause the board to cup away from that face. Conversely, a cup can be removed by wetting the inside or drying the outside. This is often accomplished by laying a board in the sun with the cupped face down.

Once a properly dried, hardwood board has been flattened and finished, bowing and twisting usually cease to be major problems. But cupping is always a danger. As a plainsawn board dries, it cups in a curve opposite to its end-grain pattern (see the drawing at right). As the board picks up moisture, it does the reverse. This is the result of differing radial and tangential shrinkage—the face of the board that was closer to the pith has more radial grain, whereas the far side has more tangential grain.

TYPES OF WOOD

There are many species of wood, but they divide into two broad groups—hardwoods and softwoods. As a general rule, hardwoods are deciduous (trees that shed their leaves annually) and softwoods are coniferous (cone-bearing trees that stay green year-round).

Furniture makers generally prefer to work with hardwoods. They are stronger, warp less, come in a greater variety of grain patterns and colors, have more dimensional stability, take a finish better and cut more cleanly. Softwoods, such as fir, pine, spruce and redwood, are most often used in the construction trades for framing, trim and finish work in houses. A softwood such as southern yellow pine is actually denser and harder than a hardwood like basswood. But in general the hardwoods are harder and the softwoods softer.

Hardwoods come from all over the world and are distinguished from one another by density, color, porosity and grain pattern. I generally work with domestic hardwoods such as cherry, maple, ash, oak, walnut and poplar. Other furniture makers prefer the elegance or flamboyance of imports like bubinga, purpleheart, imbuye, rosewood, teak, mahogany and ebony. I choose domestic hardwoods because they are readily available, relatively affordable and often easier to work, and they offer a wide enough range of colors and grain patterns to suit my design needs. Also, breathing the sawdust from imported hardwood, or skin contact with it, is more likely to cause unpleasant, and even dangerous, allergic reactions.

Many woods change color over time as a result of oxidation or exposure to sunlight. The dark brown color of American black walnut will bleach yellowish from long-term exposure to the sun. Cherry is almost orange when fresh cut, but eventually oxidizes to a rich red-brown. From tree to furniture, wood continues to interact with light, oxygen, water and heat. The character and beauty of wood never cease to be molded by the accidents of its history.

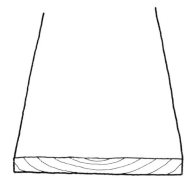

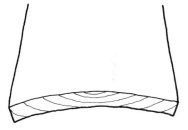

A plainsawn board cups away from the center of the tree as it dries.

MILLING LOGS

When a log goes to the sawmill, the sawyer has a number of choices to make. If the log is going to be used as solid timber, it is milled to yield either plainsawn (also called flatsawn), quartersawn or riftsawn planks. Plainsawn wood is identified by the arc pattern of its end grain and the flame pattern of its face grain. Quartersawn wood is identified by the parallel vertical strokes of its end grain and the straight parallel lines of its face grain. Riftsawn wood is similar to quartersawn, except that the end grain deviates more from the vertical.

Quartersawn and riftsawn boards are less likely to warp than plainsawn wood, and some people prefer their grain pattern. However, riftsawn and quartersawn boards are more costly to mill and create more waste than plainsawn lumber. For these reasons, most of the wood found in lumberyards is plainsawn.

PLAINSAWN AND QUARTERSAWN PLANKS

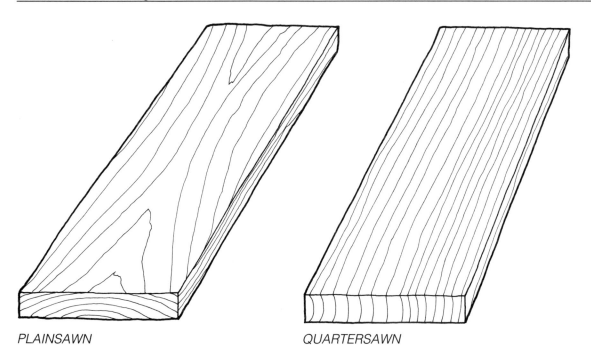

PLAINSAWN

QUARTERSAWN

TWO METHODS OF SAWING A LOG FOR SOLID TIMBER

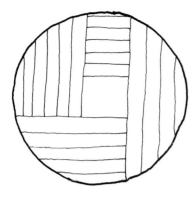

This method produces mostly plainsawn lumber.

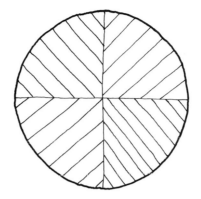

This method produces mostly quartersawn lumber.

The drawing above shows two different approaches to milling a log, depending on whether plainsawn or quartersawn wood is desired. You might think that plainsawing would be better accomplished by starting at one side and cutting parallel planks all the way through, but generally the very center of a tree is unusable because of the pith and dense knots. When milling a furniture-grade log for plainsawn lumber, the sawyer cuts in from all four sides to avoid the center, as shown.

The sawyer must also decide how thick to cut the boards. If the wood is to be sold to a lumberyard, the sawyer probably wants to end up with boards between 1 in. and 2 in. thick. A board that is going to be a specific thickness after drying must be milled oversize to allow for shrinkage in the kiln.

By the time wood gets from the sawmill to the typical lumberyard, boards from different trees within a species are intermixed. Since the color of wood varies from tree to tree, it becomes difficult to pick out matching wood for a large project. Some woodworkers solve this problem by having whole trees custom-milled at a local sawmill or with a portable chainsaw mill.

VENEER

A tremendous amount of lumber is cut for veneers, which are sheets of wood anywhere between $\frac{1}{64}$ in. and $\frac{1}{8}$ in. thick. The standard thickness for commercial veneer is between $\frac{1}{28}$ in. and $\frac{1}{32}$ in. Veneers are used industrially to make plywood and as finish surfaces on particleboard-type materials. Furniture makers use veneers as surfaces on tables and cabinets and for making curved forms through bent lamination.

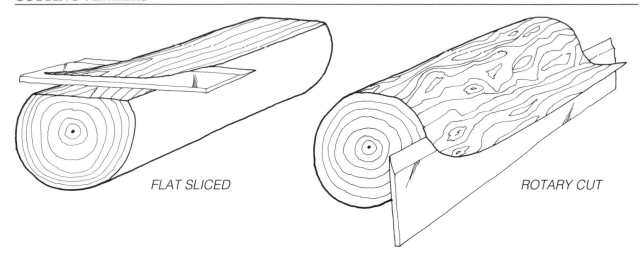

FLAT SLICED

ROTARY CUT

Veneers can be either flat-sliced or rotary-cut (see the drawing above). Rotary-cut veneers have the wandering, loopy grain seen on construction plywood. Furniture makers prefer flat-sliced veneers, since they look like solid timber. Flat-sliced veneers are often sold by the flitch, which means that the sheets have been restacked in the order they came off the tree. Working from a flitch, a furniture maker has the benefit of veneers whose grain and color match.

PLYWOOD AND PARTICLEBOARD

Much of the world's lumber harvest goes to make plywood and particleboard. Although the concept of plywood was introduced thousands of years ago, its manufacture only became practical with the development of high-quality adhesives during World War II. Plywood is made by laminating together sheets of veneer so the grain directions of adjacent pieces alternate at right angles. The long grain of each sheet prevents adjacent sheets from shrinking across their grain, and the entire assembly remains dimensionally stable. The other advantage of plywood is that, with grain running in two directions, it can't split the way solid wood does.

The thickness and number of veneers in plywood can vary. However, the number of veneers is always odd rather than even, so that the two exterior veneers will have parallel grain directions. This configuration cancels out any tendency of the plywood to cup due to changes in humidity—if one exterior sheet wants to expand and force the plywood to cup, the opposite sheet is expanding with the opposite, balancing force.

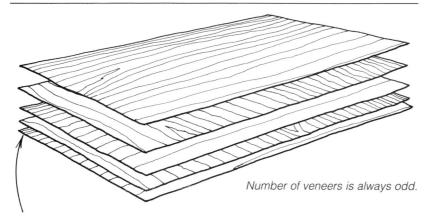

Number of veneers is always odd.

Grain direction of laminated veneer sheets alternates at 90°.

Although we will not be using plywood for the projects in this book, there are many furniture applications where plywood is a reasonable, and even desirable, solution. Cabinetmaking plywoods are distinguished from one another by the thickness, quality and species of their interior veneers. The best plywood available, Baltic birch, is made up of very thin layers of defect-free birch veneer. It is extremely stable and, no matter where you cut it, you never find a gap in the edge. Unfortunately, Baltic birch is also expensive, so I rarely use it.

Ordinary birch plywood, which is more commonly used for cabinet construction, has outside veneers of birch over thicker fir or poplar substrates. It comes in thicknesses from ⅛ in. to ¾ in. and is a good, stable product.

Other plywoods of varying thicknesses come with fine hardwood exterior veneers over fir, poplar, lauan or particleboard substrates. I sometimes buy ¼-in. hardwood-faced plywood to make drawer bottoms and cabinet backs. Thin (⅛-in.) plywood is often used when laminating large curved forms.

Man-made wood-based sheet materials are created by mixing wood chips and particles with glue. These materials go by names like particleboard, medium-density fiberboard, flakeboard and hardboard, and are used similarly to plywood. The many varieties are differentiated by the size of the wood chips and the density with which they are compacted. I don't care for these composite sheet materials; they are heavy, because of the high percentage of glue, and weak, because there is no continuity of wood fiber.

BUYING WOOD

Hardwood suppliers are relatively hard to find and sometimes sell only to professional woodworkers. When I lived on the western slope of the Rocky Mountains, I had to drive 200 miles to Denver in order to purchase hardwoods. In more populated areas, you will probably be able to find a retail hardwood dealer nearby, or a wholesale yard that also sells retail. Check the Yellow Pages under hardwoods and lumber, or call a local furniture maker, to find the best wood sources near you.

Once you have found a supplier, the ideal arrangement is to be able to look through the stacks and pick out your own boards. Many yards don't allow selection, but if you can find one that does you'll be ahead of the game.

A lumberyard dealing in softwoods and construction materials sells wood from bundles that have been cut to uniform thickness, width and length. One 10-ft. 2x4 is much like another. Hardwoods are different. A bundle of hardwood has been sorted for uniform thickness and grade, but the boards have random widths and lengths. No two boards in a bundle are exactly alike, and the quality within a single grade can vary dramatically.

Grading takes place at the sawmill, where boards are judged by width, absence of knots and proportion of sapwood. The best grade of hardwood is FAS (Firsts and Seconds), followed by Select and Better, Select, #1 Common and #2 Common, which isn't good for much except making crates and pallets. I always buy the best grade available, which is either FAS or Select and Better. But even FAS lumber doesn't always look good. I've picked through a thousand feet of FAS cherry to find only three excellent boards—the rest were bowed, too full of sapwood or too knotty. Buying walnut is particularly difficult. The quality of logs available to the mills has fallen off so much that the grading system has been revised to make what would be only a Select board in any other species an FAS board in walnut.

Hardwood is sold roughsawn or surfaced. The usual thicknesses available are 4/4 (four-quarter, which is 1 in.), 5/4, 6/4 and 8/4 (eight-quarter, which is 2 in.). Boards are called roughsawn because of the coarse surface left by the sawblade at the mill. A 4/4 roughsawn board measures a full inch in thickness. Surfaced boards, which have been run through a planer to smooth the faces, can lose up to ¼ in. of thickness in the process. A surfaced 4/4 board typically measures $^{13}/_{16}$ in. thick.

A recent innovation is hit-or-miss planing, in which the faces of a 4/4 board are skimmed down to $^{15}/_{16}$ in. at the mill to make it easier for customers at a lumberyard to read the grain, without too much loss of thickness.

Because boards surfaced at the lumberyard usually need to be remilled at home in order to be truly flat and straight, I prefer to buy roughsawn or hit-or-miss lumber, which leaves me with a thicker piece in the end. Some craftsmen take a block plane to the lumberyard in order to shave roughsawn boards for a glimpse of the grain, but yard foremen often discourage this practice. Look wood over carefully before taking it home. If it has been kiln-dried improperly it can be honeycombed with small checks that run deep inside.

CALCULATING BOARD FEET

Hardwood is priced and sold by a measurement called the board foot, which is equal to 144 cubic inches (1 square foot of a 1-in. thick board). If all measurements are in inches, board footage is calculated by the formula: thickness x width x length ÷ 144.

For example, a 12/4 board that is 6 in. wide and 40 in. long contains 5 board feet. If one of the measurements is in feet instead of inches, change the denominator to 12. For example, to determine the board footage of a plank of 8/4 cherry that is 9 in. wide and 10 ft. long, the calculation is as follows:

2 in. x 9 in. x 10 ft. ÷ 12 = 180 ÷ 12 = 15 board feet.

JOINERY

Joinery is the art of attaching one piece of wood to another. Interlocking joints, mechanical fasteners and adhesives, used singly or in combination, are the woodworker's joinery resources. Although screws and glue may serve a carpenter who is making a quick bookcase, fine furniture requires accurately cut interlocking joinery. The joint that holds a stretcher to a chair leg, or a drawer side to a drawer front, must be able to withstand the thousand stresses of daily use as well as cope with the seasonal movement of wood over generations.

Many modern joinery techniques were practiced thousands of years ago by the ancient Egyptians, then forgotten in Europe until the late Middle Ages. After all these centuries, mortise and tenons and dovetails are still the preferred methods for joining wood. The only real advance in the joiner's art has been the mid-twentieth century development of reliable glues.

A joint is considered to have mechanical strength to the extent that the pieces of wood interlock. It has glue strength to the extent that edge grain contacts edge grain for a good glue bond. Sometimes mechanical strength or glue strength alone forms a sufficient joint, sometimes both are required.

The major factor the woodworker must cope with when joining wood together is wood movement. Also important is the propensity of glue to bond well on edge grain but poorly on end grain.

COPING WITH WOOD MOVEMENT

Wood movement becomes a problem when two pieces of wood are joined together so the cross-grain expansion and contraction of one is inhibited by the long-grain stability of the other. A common breadboard provides a good example.

As shown in the drawing below, the grain of the center board runs perpendicular to the grain of the cap pieces, and the boards meet in tongue-and-groove joints. One cap is pegged in place in the middle, the other is pegged at the ends. No glue has been used.

Now, let's consider what will happen if the breadboard is introduced into a drier climate. The center board will want to shrink across its grain. The end with the single peg will have no problem. Shrinkage will take place toward the fixed point, and the only noticeable effect will be that the outside edges of the breadboard no longer line up.

The other end of the breadboard is a different story. Since the cap piece stays constant in length, the two pegs can't get any closer together. As a result, the center board is prevented from shrinking and will most likely split in the center to relieve the tension of pulling toward two fixed points. If the cap pieces had been spot-glued at the same locations, instead of pegged, the same results would have

PROBLEMS OF WOOD MOVEMENT

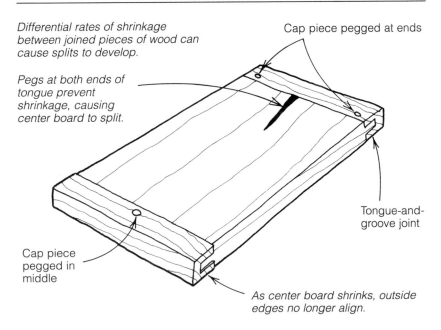

Differential rates of shrinkage between joined pieces of wood can cause splits to develop.

Pegs at both ends of tongue prevent shrinkage, causing center board to split.

Cap piece pegged at ends

Tongue-and-groove joint

Cap piece pegged in middle

As center board shrinks, outside edges no longer align.

occurred. If the caps had been glued along the entire length of the tongue and groove, stress would have occurred as with the two end pegs, and splits may have developed.

Cabinet doors and tabletops present another challenge in coping with wood movement: Given wood's propensity for cupping and movement across the grain, how do you keep a wide expanse of wood flat and stable?

One traditional solution is board-and-batten construction. Several boards are placed edge to edge with two or three battens attached crossways to keep them flat (see the drawing at right). If the boards haven't been glued to one another, they can be screwed to the battens and left to shrink and expand independently of each other. The battens will hold them reasonably flat, and lapping the edges of the boards over one another will prevent see-through gaps between them.

When the boards are glued together to form one wide board, however, allowance must be made for expansion and contraction across the entire width. This is commonly done by cutting slots in the battens that allow the screw shanks to move with the board, as shown in the drawing below.

BOARD-AND-BATTEN CONSTRUCTION

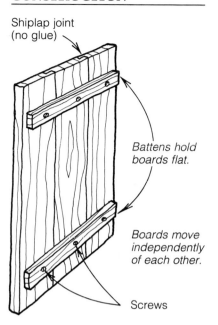

Shiplap joint (no glue)

Battens hold boards flat.

Boards move independently of each other.

Screws

ALLOWING FOR WOOD MOVEMENT

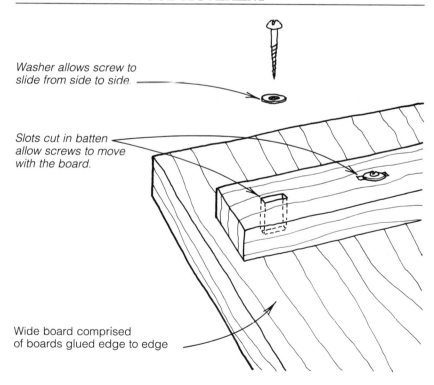

Washer allows screw to slide from side to side.

Slots cut in batten allow screws to move with the board.

Wide board comprised of boards glued edge to edge

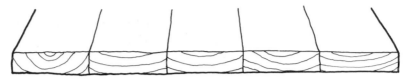

ALL GROWTH-RING CURVES THE SAME

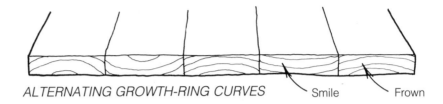

ALTERNATING GROWTH-RING CURVES   Smile   Frown

FRAME-AND-PANEL CONSTRUCTION

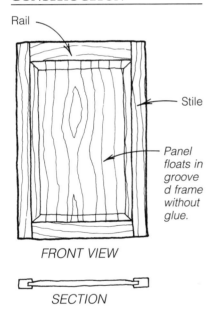

Rail

Stile

Panel floats in grooved frame without glue.

FRONT VIEW

SECTION

The end-grain orientation of edge-glued boards affects the movement of the entire panel, since wood tends to cup in the direction opposite the curve of the growth rings. Two strategies for assembling a tabletop to minimize cupping are shown in the drawing above. The first strategy is to glue all the boards together with their growth rings "smiling," and affix each batten with a single screw at the center. Over time, the top will try to frown as one cohesive unit, but the screws will prevent the center from lifting.

The second strategy to minimize cupping is to alternate the growth-ring curves: smile, frown, smile, frown, and so on. Although the boards may cup, they will tend to cancel each other out so the overall surface stays fairly flat. A third strategy is to place the best looking side of each board up (my usual method) and let the growth rings fall where they may.

A more sophisticated method for making wide, flat wood surfaces is frame-and-panel construction (see the drawing at left). The vertical components of the frame are called "stiles" and the horizontal components are "rails." Because the length of the grain runs around the perimeter of the frame, only slight changes in dimension can occur as a result of changes in moisture content. The panel floats in a groove, without glue, so it is free to shrink and expand but cannot cup.

TYPES OF JOINTS

There are three basic applications for joinery in furniture making (see the drawing below). The first is where pieces of wood meet edge to edge, with their grain running parallel, as in a panel or a tabletop. The second is where the end of one board runs into the edge of another, as in a door frame. The third is where two pieces of wood meet end to end to form a corner, as in carcase construction (boxes, chests and drawers).

In panel construction, no mechanical joint is needed if the edges of the boards meet cleanly. Glue creates a bond between the parallel wood fibers that is stronger than the natural bond provided by lignin, so the joint becomes the strongest part of the whole. Some woodworkers insert dowels, splines or biscuits in an edge joint, but these serve mainly to align the boards for gluing.

Fame construction is typified by the joint between a rail and a stile. The three main methods of assembling this joint are with a mortise and tenon, dowel, and tongue and groove. The mortise and tenon is the best joint in this category, since it provides extensive mechanical and glue strength.

In carcase construction, the top-of-the-line joint is the dovetail. Second-best alternatives are tongue and groove, spline and box joints, followed by dowels, nails and screws.

You may not always choose the strongest joint. Sometimes the look you desire, the time available or the tools at hand make a lesser joint preferable. For example, although dovetails are stronger and more durable, box joints are often adequate for carcase assembly and they are more economical to make in production.

An illustrated glossary of basic wood joints follows. Projects 2 and 3 provide detailed instructions for cutting the two most important joints: the mortise and tenon (pp. 101-115) and the dovetail (pp. 117-125).

BASIC JOINERY APPLICATIONS

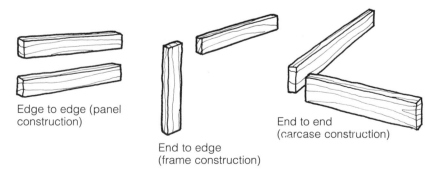

Edge to edge (panel construction)

End to edge (frame construction)

End to end (carcase construction)

MORTISE AND TENON

A mortise is a hole, usually rectangular, cut in a piece of wood. A tenon is a tongue, projecting from another piece of wood, made to fit in the mortise. Variations on the mortise and tenon include blind or through tenons, the bridle joint, and the haunched tenon. A blind tenon is invisible after the joint is assembled, because the mortise is cut in the wood from only one side. A through tenon remains visible after assembly, since the mortise is cut completely through.

MORTISE AND TENON

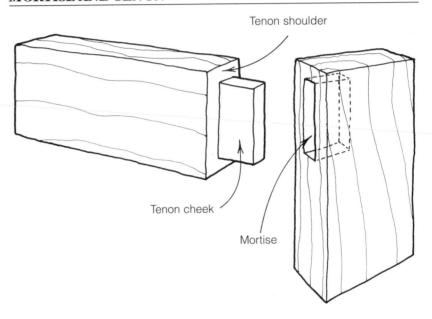

Tenon shoulder

Tenon cheek

Mortise

TENON VARIATIONS

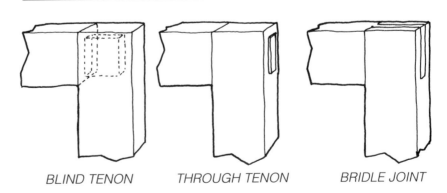

BLIND TENON   *THROUGH TENON*   *BRIDLE JOINT*

A bridle joint is essentially an open mortise and tenon. The mortise is open on three sides, and the tenon is exposed on two sides after assembly.

A haunch adds strength to the mortise-and-tenon joint by creating extra mechanical interlock and edge-grain glue surface. Often, haunches are employed for the more practical purpose of filling a groove that has been ploughed through a door stile to hold a panel. Otherwise, the groove would show as a square hole in the edge of the door.

The mechanical strength of a properly proportioned mortise and tenon is considerable. If the tenon is glued, pinned or wedged in place, the joint will not pull, twist or rock apart. A well-proportioned mortise and tenon also offers extensive glue strength—the cheeks of the tenon meet the sides of the mortise edge grain to edge grain, though the grains run at right angles to one another. At first glance, we might expect the differential movement between the cheeks of a tenon and the sides of a mortise to compromise the joint over time. In practice, unless a tenon is particularly wide, there is no problem. In a well-cut mortise and tenon, only a portion of the glued surfaces have to stay bonded in order to maintain the integrity of the joint; most stress is handled by the joint's mechanical properties.

The rule for proportion is that the length of the tenon should be at least twice its thickness. In frames, thickness is often determined by the rule that the shoulder on either side of a mortise should be as thick as the mortise itself. Shoulders that are too thin are liable to break out under stress.

The width of a tenon can vary quite a bit, depending on the width of the rail from which it protrudes. However, if a tenon gets too wide, a breadboard effect comes into play; differential shrinkage between the cheeks of the tenon and the sides of the mortise can cause glue failure or splitting in the joint. If a tenon must be more than 3 in. wide, substitute a series of smaller haunched tenons. Multiple tenons are not a perfect solution, but they do spread the stress of shrinkage more evenly.

A related joint is the round mortise and tenon, which is, in effect, like a dowel joint, and suffers the defects of that joint, as described on p. 26.

INSERTED TENONS

An inserted tenon has matching mortises cut in both sides of the joint and a separate piece of wood (a "loose tenon") milled to fit tightly between them.

In strength and function, an inserted tenon is essentially equivalent to a standard mortise-and-tenon joint. Inserted tenons are often used in commercial shops to save time and money on production runs.

HAUNCHED TENON WITH GROOVED STILE

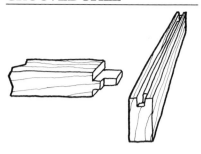

MULTIPLE MORTISE AND TENON

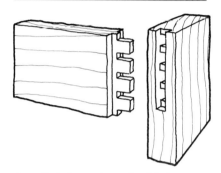

A multiple tenon is preferable to a single tenon more than 3 in. wide.

INSERTED TENON

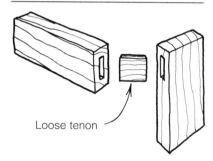

Loose tenon

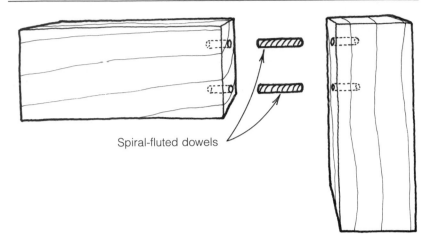

Spiral-fluted dowels

DOWEL HOLE

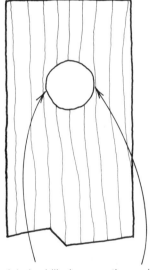

A hole drilled across the grain provides edge-grain glue surface only at sides.

DOWEL JOINTS

The dowel joint is probably the most common method of joinery used by woodworkers and manufacturers, but popularity should not be confused with quality. The dowel joint has inherent defects that limit its effectiveness. In fact, if you've seen manufactured chairs and tables with the legs falling off, you've probably noticed that they are joined with dowels.

Dowel joints are popular because they are easy to make. Matching holes are drilled in two pieces of wood and a dowel pin is glued between them. Unfortunately, a hole drilled across the grain provides very little edge-grain glue surface (see the drawing at left). To make matters worse, dowels lose their round shape over time because of differing rates of radial and tangential shrinkage; they become oval pegs in round holes.

In spite of their limitations, dowels are a good choice in some situations, including:
- joining together a prototype that doesn't have to last,
- joining parts of a continuous chair arm, where end grain butts against end grain,
- lining up boards while gluing a tabletop together,
- joining the sides of a cabinet to an overhanging top and bottom.

As with a mortise and tenon, the depth of a dowel hole should be at least twice its diameter. Dowels of various diameters can be purchased at lumberyards and hardware stores in the form of long rods or precut pins. Of the two, precut pins have been milled to more accurate diameters and have spiral or straight grooves cut along their lengths as glue channels. The channels allow glue to escape from the hole as the dowel is driven in; otherwise, hydraulic pressure could split the wood.

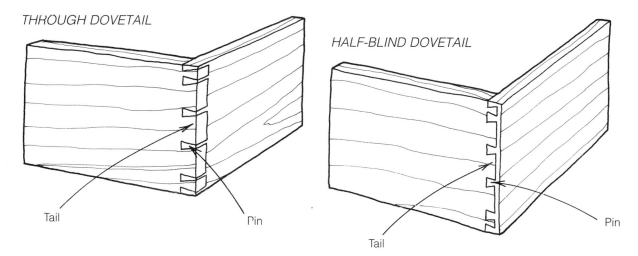

THROUGH DOVETAIL

HALF-BLIND DOVETAIL

Tail

Pin

Tail

Pin

DOVETAILS

Dovetails are the classic joint for solid-wood carcase construction. They create strong mechanical interlock and plenty of edge-grain contact for glue. Because dovetails are used only where the ends of two boards meet, wood movement is never a problem—the boards move in unison.

There are three basic dovetail variations: through, half-blind and blind. The choice of which to use is generally an aesthetic one. I have never had occasion to cut blind dovetails, which are much more difficult to make and don't show after the joint is assembled.

BOX JOINT

The box joint, or finger joint, is used for the same applications as dovetails. It is a strong joint, with plenty of edge-grain glue contact, but seems to be rarely used in fine furniture. Perhaps this is because the box joint is best suited to machine production and conveys little of the sense of hand-made quality that a dovetail imparts.

BOX JOINT

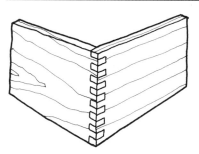

TONGUE-AND-GROOVE JOINTS

The tongue-and-groove joint has many applications, as in flooring, siding and other situations where boards meet edge to edge.

Though it can be considered a form of overkill, tongue and groove is occasionally used in place of a simple edge joint for tabletops, since it provides extra glue surface within the joint, a mechanical bond and a surefire means of lining boards up during assembly.

Tongue-and-groove joinery is also used for carcase construction. It doesn't form a first-rate corner joint in solid wood, because the intersections are all end grain to edge grain, resulting in weak glue bonds. However, tongue and groove is a great joint for plywood carcases, where layers of edge grain are exposed in every surface of the joint.

For commercial cabinets and doors, rails are often attached to stiles with a tongue-and-groove joint. This is greatly inferior to a mortise-and-tenon joint, since there is relatively little mechanical and glue strength. I recently used 6-in. lag bolts to reassemble a fairly new exterior door because the original tongue-and-groove joinery had failed to hold it together.

TONGUE-AND-GROOVE EDGE JOINT

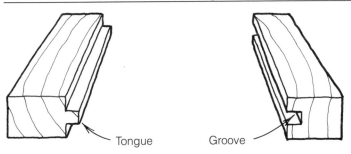

Tongue   Groove

TONGUE-AND-GROOVE CARCASE JOINT

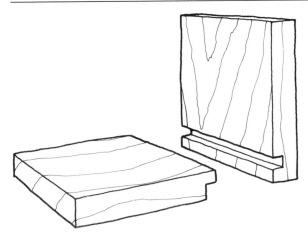

SPLINE JOINTS

Spline joints are similar to tongue and groove, except that the tongue (spline) is a separate piece of wood that fits into grooves cut in both sides of the joint. Splines are useful in most of the same situations as tongue and groove. Additionally, they are used to provide mechanical strength, glue surface and registration for mitered corners.

The grain direction of a spline is crucial. It should be oriented to shrink and expand in harmony with the grain of the grooves. For a splined edge joint, the grain should run along the spline's length. For a splined miter joint, the grain should run across the spline.

SPLINED EDGE JOINT

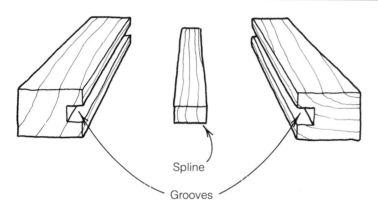

Spline

Grooves

SPLINED MITER JOINTS

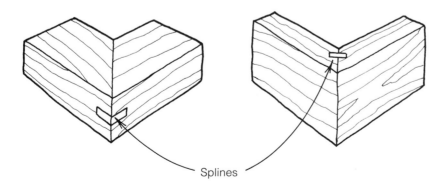

Splines

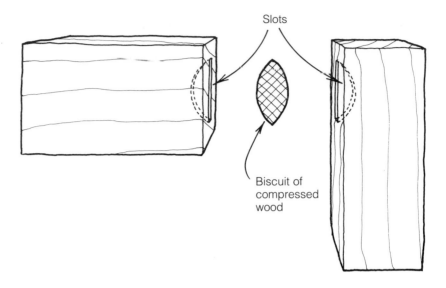

Slots

Biscuit of
compressed
wood

BISCUIT JOINERY

Biscuit (or plate) joinery is a recent technology that works like an inserted tenon and combines aspects of spline and dowel joinery. Biscuits can be an efficient substitute for splines, dowels, and tenons in applications as varied as edge-gluing boards, joining mitered corners and assembling frames.

A biscuit joiner has a small circular sawblade that is used to cut matching slots in two pieces of wood. The biscuit inserted between them is a thin, fish-shaped piece of compressed wood. As moisture is absorbed during glue-up, biscuits expand tightly in the slots.

Some contemporary furniture makers have taken to biscuits as an across-the-board substitute for mortise-and-tenon joinery. Others, including myself, are skeptical as to whether biscuits provide sufficient meat to form durable joints where any degree of long-term stress is involved, as in a chair or table frame.

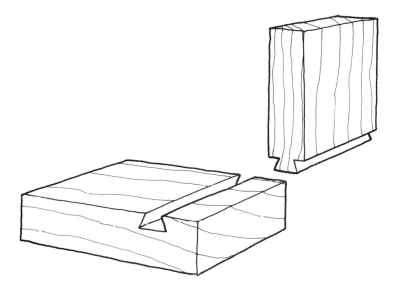

SLIDING DOVETAILS

The sliding dovetail can be used to attach battens to boards, drawer sides to overhanging faces, and dividers to the insides of cabinets, among other things. Mechanically, it is a very strong joint. Glue strength varies, depending on the grain orientation between the boards. If the grain of the dovetail runs crosswise to that of the host piece, the joint should be glued in only one spot to allow for shrinkage and expansion.

SCREWS AND NAILS

A friend who repairs antique furniture first explained to me the incompatibility of screws and wood. Over and over, he finds old furniture that has fallen apart because the screws have worked loose. The wood in a screw hole gradually wears away as it rubs against the metal of the screw with each season's expansion and contraction.

In furniture built to last, the few legitimate uses for screws include attaching a door or tabletop to battens, mounting hinges and hardware, or perhaps putting a plywood back on a solid-wood cabinet.

With all that said, screws are an indispensable part of the furniture workshop. They are invaluable for assembling mock-ups, jigs and fixtures. I keep a supply of drywall screws on hand for just these uses—they rarely break, and the Phillips-head slot makes them easy to drive with an electric drill.

Nails are more suited to carpentry than to fine furniture making. They provide a dubious long-term mechanical bond, and the movement of wood over time will gradually back a nail out of its hole. The main use for nails in my shop is to make jigs and fixtures.

INTRODUCTION TO
WOODWORKING MACHINES

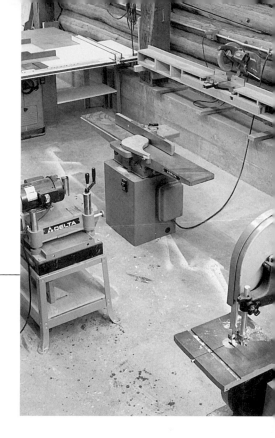

Machinery has become such an accepted part of the modern workshop that the meaning of the phrase "hand-made furniture" has changed. Once used to describe furniture constructed entirely with hand tools, "hand-made" now signifies furniture built by an individual craftsman rather than a factory. No one complains that the modern craftsman mills rough boards to thickness with electrically powered table saws, jointers and planers instead of a rip saw and hand planes. Machines are simply more efficient for milling lumber.

It would be wrong, however, to draw the conclusion that machines and power tools are an across-the-board replacement for hand tools. In fact, quite the opposite is true. There is little a machine can do that a craftsman skilled in the use of hand tools can't do as well or better (albeit more slowly), but there are many situations where the work of hand tools can't even be attempted with machinery.

The best approach to acquiring woodworking craftsmanship is to begin by mastering the use of hand skills for cutting joinery, hand planes for flattening and smoothing wood, and machinery for basic milling operations. Later, with confidence in your hand skills, you may choose to substitute machine work for hand work in situations where it will save time without compromising quality.

The basic stationary machines for furniture making are the table saw, bandsaw, jointer, thickness planer, drill press, grinder and lathe. Other machines that are useful but less essential include the radial-arm saw, disc/belt sander and chopsaw. The most commonly used hand-held power tools are the router, drill and various sanders.

Although this book emphasizes hand skills and explains how to work lumber without power tools, it generally assumes that the reader has access to basic woodworking machines for the process of milling rough lumber to finished thickness, width and length. If you don't have your own machinery, you can often obtain access to it through the continuing education program at your local community college. You might also look for shared workshop space nearby.

This chapter presents the basic woodworking machines and power tools, explaining what they do and how to use them safely. More detailed, step-by-step instructions on using the table saw, jointer and thickness planer are offered in the chapter "Milling a Board Four-Square" (pp. 83-99). If you already have your own machinery and feel comfortable using it, you might look at this chapter as a review. If you are just learning to use machinery, a prudent addition to reading this material would be to find some hands-on instruction.

SHOP SAFETY

Any discussion of woodworking machinery should begin with shop safety. Woodworking machines are made to cut, slice, chop, abrade, drill and shave materials that are considerably harder than human flesh. Machines are dangerous when used carelessly and wonderfully helpful when used well.

Wherever woodworkers gather, stories of accidents and near-misses come up sooner or later. A Danish furniture maker in Philadelphia told me of coming to work one morning and finding fingers strewn about the table saw. Apparently, at the end of the previous day, his partner's German shepherd had jumped against the man's back just as he was making a cut, forcing the man's hand through the blade.

I've seen a couple of bad accidents myself, and both were the result of carelessness by the injured person. Perhaps our terminology is wrong. "Accident" implies that the injured person is a "victim" of circumstances beyond his or her control; in most cases it may be more appropriate to say that the "perpetrator" suffers the consequences of his or her own carelessness.

SAFETY IN THE SHOP

Consciousness of safety is the first requirement of good craftsmanship. Ten important shop safety procedures are listed below. Safety tips specific to each woodworking machine are discussed in the relevant sections.

1. Wear hearing and eye protection when using saws, routers, sanders and other equipment. I know woodworkers who are kept awake at night by the sound of imaginary routers because they worked without headphones or earplugs for too many years. To keep dust and splinters out of my eyes, I rely on the large plastic lenses of my prescription glasses, but they are barely adequate. I strongly recommend wearing safety glasses, goggles or a face shield when using power equipment.

2. Keep your workshop clean and neat so you won't trip over a scrap of wood or an extension cord at an inopportune moment.

3. Tie up long hair, and don't wear loose clothing or jewelry. I met a woman whose hair had caught in a planer during a college woodworking course. Fortunately for her, the instructor was there to disengage the clutch instantly; otherwise her scalp would have been ripped off.

4. Don't use machinery when you're tired or have consumed alcohol. Woodworking equipment is dangerous enough when you are fully alert, so why increase the odds against you? My personal rule is not to use machinery after dark, when I assume I'll be more tired.

5. Focus on what you are doing at all times, and take a break if your mind starts to wander. You are most likely to have accidents when performing the same operation over and over again.

6. If you're not comfortable making a particular cut or aren't sure it's safe, get advice or help before you try it. Find a friendly professional woodworker to ask.

7. Keep sawblades sharp. The harder you have to push, the less control you have.

8. Be prepared for accidents. Consider these questions: Where are your telephone, your first-aid kit and the nearest person who can help? Can you give clear directions to your shop over the telephone? Are you familiar with basic first-aid and tourniquet procedures?

9. If a serious injury occurs, call 911 for an ambulance rather than have a friend drive you to the hospital. What would your friend do if you went into shock on the highway?

10. If you should be so unfortunate as to sever any fingers, take them with you to the hospital in case they can be reattached. Severed fingers should be wrapped in gauze and soaked in a cup of salty water that is kept cold over ice. The fingers should not make direct contact with the ice.

HEALTH CONCERNS

Breathing sawdust isn't healthy; it can be allergenic, toxic and carcinogenic. The sawdust from some imported woods, including teak, is particularly harmful and is known to cause skin rashes and respiratory problems. Several studies have shown that woodworkers have a high rate of nasal cancer.

Because even a little sawdust clogs my sinuses and aggravates my allergies, I try to wear a mask whenever I make dust, whether with machinery or sandpaper or sweeping the floor. Masks range from thin paper with an elastic strap to thick rubber with a replaceable, toxic-fume-proof filter. Heavy-duty masks are generally unpleasant to wear, so some compromise needs to be made between efficiency and comfort. I find that a two-strap paper mask with a flexible metal nose bridge seals out sawdust well and is comfortable enough for constant use.

Some of the solvents and finishes used in furniture finishing are also allergenic, toxic and carcinogenic. Petroleum distillates in commercial oil finishes, naphtha and benzene are all suspect. Over many years of use I've become allergic to turpentine, with which I formerly thinned oil finishes on the theory that it was a "natural" product and therefore safe. Now I use mineral spirits, which at least doesn't make me sneeze.

Because many solvents can be absorbed by breathing or through the skin, it is a good idea to wear rubber gloves and a toxic-vapor mask when working with them.

THE TABLE SAW

The table saw is the first piece of major equipment most woodworkers purchase. This versatile tool can be used to make straight cuts along the length of a board (ripping), across the width (crosscutting) or at any angle, including 45° (mitering). The table saw can also be used to cut grooves and various types of joints, such as the box joint, tenon, bridle joint and tongue and groove.

A table saw should be sturdily built with a strong motor. An underpowered, undersized saw won't handle hardwoods satisfactorily. Variables to consider in purchasing a saw include blade diameter, voltage and horsepower.

Table saws are sized according to the diameter of the blade they take. Common sizes are 8 in., 10 in. and 12 in., though larger and smaller ones exist. The standard among furniture makers is a 10-in. table saw. Fully raised at 90°, a 10-in. blade will cut through about 3 in. of wood.

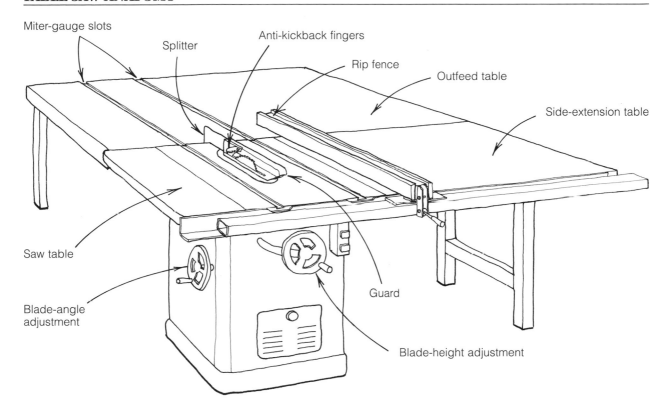

Miter-gauge slots

Splitter

Anti-kickback fingers

Rip fence

Outfeed table

Side-extension table

Saw table

Blade-angle adjustment

Guard

Blade-height adjustment

A 10-in. table saw should have a motor of at least 3 hp, wired for 220-volt single phase or for three-phase electricity. Normal 120-volt house current doesn't always have enough kick to power a sawblade through a 2-in. piece of oak, especially if the freshly cut end pinches the blade.

Before using a new table saw, check to be sure that the table is mounted in line with the blade. This can be done by putting a long straightedge against the side of the fully raised blade and measuring to see that it is parallel with the miter-gauge slots that run through the table. If the blade and the table are out of alignment, the top of the saw can be loosened and repositioned.

A basic table saw can be greatly improved by the addition of auxiliary tables and a good rip fence. An extension table to the side and an outfeed table behind the saw make it easier and safer to cut large sheets of plywood and long boards, especially if you work alone. You can buy ready-made extension tables for some saws, but they are also easy to build yourself. The width of the side-extension table is often determined by the capacity of the rip fence. In my shop the extension table is wide enough to accommodate a 53-in. capacity rip fence, and the outfeed table extends 42 in. beyond the saw table.

A rip fence is used when sawing a board along its length.

A rip fence is used when sawing a board to width or thickness along its length. Once upon a time, table saws came with mediocre rip fences supplied by the manufacturers, and that was that. But in the past 15 years, independent companies have introduced improved rip fences, and some table-saw manufacturers now provide them as standard equipment. A rip fence should be sturdy, adjust and remove easily, and have faces that are truly perpendicular to the table. I particularly like the fence system made by Biesemeyer.

Woodworkers argue about whether a rip fence should be set exactly parallel to the sawblade or a hair wider at the far end. The hair-wider school wants to be doubly sure that wood doesn't bind between the sawblade and the rip fence during a cut. When wood does bind it either burns from friction or kicks back dangerously. In my experience, either setting seems to work fine.

Crosscutting is done with the aid of a miter gauge or sliding table. Crosscutting freehand against the rip fence may be the most common and dangerous mistake that beginners make. Never do it! If you crosscut a board with one end against the rip fence and a corner pulls just a hair off the fence, the other end of the board will jam into the blade and come flying back at you. The hand holding the board may be drawn into the blade before you can react.

A miter gauge (left) or a sliding table (above) should always be used when crosscutting on the table saw.

A wooden fence attached to the face of the miter gauge increases its utility.

A miter gauge comes as standard equipment with most table saws. It slides in miter-gauge slots on either side of the blade and can be set to cut any angle up to 45°. Lengthening the face of the gauge by attaching a straight piece of wood will increase its accuracy, control and versatility. Another trick is to line the face of the guide with sandpaper to keep wood from sliding while being cut. Attach the sandpaper (180 or 220 grit) with a spray adhesive.

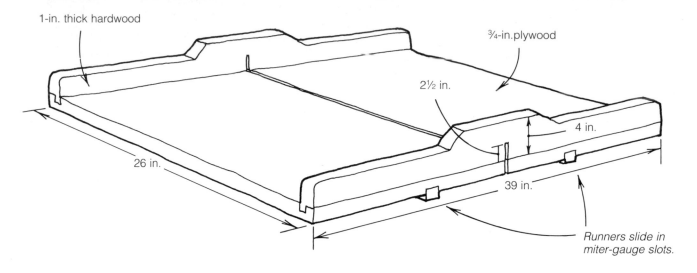

1-in. thick hardwood

¾-in. plywood

2½ in.

4 in.

26 in.

39 in.

Runners slide in miter-gauge slots.

The best accessory for accurate and safe crosscutting is a sliding table. Unlike the miter gauge, which runs in one slot and can wobble a bit, a well-made sliding table rides securely in both miter gauge slots and is designed to handle longer and wider stock. Sliding tables are available commercially or can be made at home. When using a sliding table it is important to keep your hands away from the slot where the blade comes out the back as you push through.

Sawblades available for table saws include rip, crosscut, combination, dado and plywood blades. They vary from one another according to the type, set, number and spacing of the teeth. There are also choices to make between carbide and steel teeth, and between standard and thin-kerf blades. Buy good-quality sawblades. This is not the place to save money. A good blade is balanced and set to give a cleaner, smoother cut; a bad blade is misery to work with.

In general, carbide is better than steel because it stays sharp much longer. The only situation in which I prefer steel is when cutting wood that may contain nails or screws. Better to ruin a cheap blade than a good one.

Thin-kerf blades, which leave a kerf just under $3/32$ in. wide instead of ⅛ in. or wider, are fairly new on the market. They can be better for ripping than regular blades because they remove less wood and don't have to work as hard. Standard-thickness blades are perfectly adequate, however.

Most of the time I leave a combination blade on my table saw, because it can rip, crosscut or miter. I switch to a rip blade when I have a lot of ripping to do at one time, but I rarely use a crosscut blade.

Dado blades are used to cut dadoes (flat-bottomed grooves cut through a board) and rabbets (grooves cut along an edge). The better type of dado blade has seven component blades that can be assembled to cut any thickness from ¼ in. to ¹³⁄₁₆ in. by sixteenths. The inferior kind, commonly known as "the wobbler," is a single blade whose teeth adjust on a cam to cut any width from ¼ in. to ¾ in.

Over time, pitch from wood adheres to the sides of a blade and reduces cutting efficiency. To remove pitch, soak the blade overnight in a plastic tub, in a solution of household lye and water. (Be sure to read the safety instructions on the lye container.) In the morning, you will be able to remove the pitch with a sponge or toothbrush. Baking soda and oven cleaner can also be used to remove pitch.

Sawblades should be changed with the saw unplugged. The nut that holds the blade on the arbor need only be hand-tight; because the arbor thread is reversed, the rotation of the blade has a self-tightening effect.

SAFETY EQUIPMENT

More accidents occur on the table saw than on any other woodworking machine. Accordingly, many different kinds of safety devices have been developed to keep your hands away from the sawblade and to prevent the saw from throwing wood back at you. Kickback, which can be strong enough to send a 2x4 through a wall 20 ft. away, is usually caused by wood binding between the blade and the fence. It can also result when the ends of a board pinch together as they pass the sawblade, or from careless operation of the saw. The two dangers of kickback are, first, that the returning board can hit you, and, second, that if you are holding the wood with one hand beyond the sawblade, your hand can be drawn back across the blade before you have a chance to let go.

Safety equipment for the table saw includes hold-downs, anti-kickback fingers, splitters, blade guards and push sticks. Many new table saws come with a splitter, anti-kickback fingers and a blade guard in an integrated unit as standard equipment. The splitter (see the top drawing on p. 37), also known as a riving knife, is a narrow piece of metal rising just behind the sawblade that keeps the kerf from closing on the blade as wood re-tensions itself during a cut. Anti-kickback fingers are pieces of metal that ride over the board as it passes the sawblade. Their teeth allow the wood to move in one direction only.

The most common type of blade guard is a clear plastic cover that lifts as wood passes underneath. It does a good job of keeping your hands from the blade, but also has some disadvantages. The guard can make it difficult to see the blade meet the wood; it gets in the way when ripping narrow strips, and has to be removed entirely when a sliding table is in use.

SAFETY TIPS FOR THE TABLE SAW

1. Never let go of a piece of wood in the middle of a cut, lest it end up in your face or groin. Push wood through until it passes the blade entirely.

2. Keep wood firmly against the fence when ripping.

3. Make sure that your saw is equipped with the right safety equipment, including a splitter and anti-kickback fingers.

4. Set blade height just a tooth above the wood.

5. When crosscutting or mitering, always use a miter guide or sliding table, not the rip fence.

6. Use a push stick for ripping.

7. Unplug the saw when changing blades.

8. Keep blades sharp.

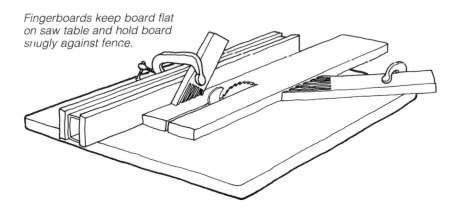

Fingerboards keep board flat on saw table and hold board snugly against fence.

PUSH-STICK DESIGNS

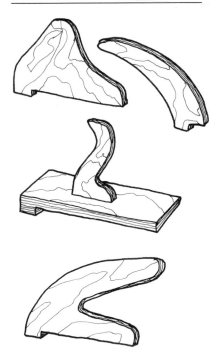

Hold-downs are devices that exert pressure to keep wood against the saw table or the fence during a rip cut. One commercially sold version is a plastic wheel that attaches to the fence. The homemade version, called a fingerboard or featherboard, is a piece of wood with parallel saw kerfs cut into one end to leave thin, flexible fingers. I have never had occasion to use hold-downs, but circumstances in which they would be helpful include ripping thin flexible stock and production milling where many boards of identical dimension are going to be ripped at the same setting.

Push sticks keep your hands out of danger when ripping on a table saw (or using a jointer). It is especially important to use them when ripping wood to less than 3 in. in width. Push sticks can be cut in a variety of shapes and are usually made out of plywood, since it won't split at an inopportune moment the way solid wood might. I prefer push-stick designs that extend forward over the wood to hold it down at the same time as they push it forward.

For certain types of cuts, standard safety equipment gets in the way and must be removed. As a general rule, though, it is best to use every safety precaution available, when possible.

THE BANDSAW

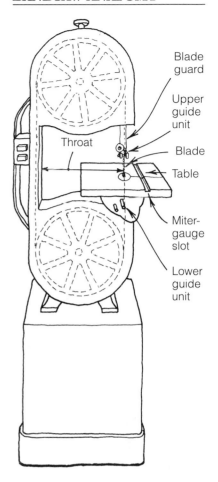

If I could have only one piece of machinery in my workshop, it would be a bandsaw. This versatile tool can do anything from the brute work of resawing a 6-in. hardwood beam into planks to the delicate work of cutting the curves for a cabriole leg.

I often use the bandsaw in situations where others might use a table saw, because the bandsaw is friendlier and safer. A prime example is ripping rough lumber to approximate width at the start of the milling process (see pp. 86-88). Bowed or cupped boards that might tend to jam or kick back on a table saw cut smoothly on the bandsaw. On the other hand, the table saw is definitely better suited to making straight, square finish cuts at the conclusion of the milling process.

A bandsaw consists of a continuous ribbon of sawblade held under tension between two (or sometimes three) wheels, one of which is driven by a motor. The blade runs through upper and lower guide units made up of blocks or bearings to either side and a bearing behind; the upper unit also has a blade guard attached. Bandsaw tables can tilt to make angled cuts up to and beyond 45°.

Bandsaws are specified according to the diameter of their wheels. The standard size for amateur and small professional shops is 14 in. The wheel diameter on a two-wheel bandsaw determines the "throat" width—the horizontal distance between the cutting blade and the body of the saw. A 14-in. Delta bandsaw has a 13¾-in. throat. The other significant measurement, the maximum thickness a bandsaw will cut, is determined by how high the upper guide unit lifts off the table. On a 14-in. Delta bandsaw this distance is 6⅜ in.

Bandsaw blades are distinguished by width, number of teeth per inch and tooth form. Narrower blades cut sharper curves; wider blades are better at cutting straight lines and resawing. A 14-in. bandsaw takes blades from ¹⁄₁₆ in. to ¾ in. in width, though ½ in. is the widest most people use.

Blades with fewer teeth cut thick stock better because they heat up less from friction and carry dust out of the kerf more efficiently. For wood up to 2 in. thick, blades with six teeth per inch are recommended. For wood from 2 in. to 4 in. thick, use four teeth per inch. For sawing through more than 4 in. of wood you may want to use a blade with only two or three teeth per inch, though I've found that a four-tooth blade works fine.

There are two tooth forms used for woodcutting bandsaw blades: hook tooth and skip tooth. Hook teeth are more aggressive, remove a wider kerf and are better for cutting hardwoods. Skip teeth have a larger gullet, clear chips better and are preferred for cutting softwoods. Skip teeth cut more smoothly than hook teeth. I usually keep a four-tooth hook blade on my saw, changing to a six-tooth hook or skip only when I need a smoother cut.

Unlike the table saw, much work on the bandsaw is done freehand, without fences or a miter gauge. When you do set up a fence, perhaps for resawing veneers from solid stock, there is an important trick to know called "setting the drift." A bandsaw blade rarely cuts in line with the edge of a bandsaw table. With the fence set parallel to the table (like a table-saw fence), the flexible blade tends to wander to one side, slicing the wood either too thick or too thin.

To set the drift, mark a straight line parallel to the edge of a scrap board and then find the angle at which you must push the board through to saw along the line. This is the angle at which you should set the fence for perfect resawing.

THE JOINTER

The jointer is used to make one face of a board flat and straight or one edge of a board flat, straight and square to a face. It consists of two long flat tables flanking a high-speed cylindrical cutterhead, a fence, a motor and a blade guard. The cutterhead usually holds three parallel steel knives, though other configurations are possible. Jointers are specified according to the length of their knives, which determines the width of board they can handle. Common sizes for home and small professional shops are 6 in. and 8 in. Wider is better—shops that handle timber for tabletops and cabinets may have jointers 18 in. wide and more.

The outfeed table of a jointer is set tangent to the apex of the knives' rotation (see the drawing on the facing page). The infeed table is set lower, determining the depth of cut. I take off less than $\frac{1}{16}$ in. per pass so as not to strain the machine.

Wood should be fed through the jointer so that it cuts with the grain. If a board has grain running in two different directions, the best way to minimize tearout is to take very fine cuts, make sure the knives are sharp and feed the wood slowly.

When milling a gnarly piece of wood that will require many passes to become flat, I often disregard grain direction and flip the board end for end for the first several cuts. Flipping the board avoids the occasional problem of having more wood taken off one side of the board than the other by knives that are set unevenly in relation to the jointer tables.

"Snipe" is a common problem with jointed boards. It occurs when the outfeed table is set incorrectly, below the apex of the knives' rotation. As a board leaves the support of the infeed table at the

The jointer is used to establish a flat face and perpendicular edge.

USING THE JOINTER

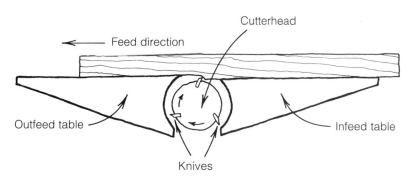

conclusion of each pass it drops to the level of the outfeed table, resulting in the last 2 in. or so becoming slightly thinner than the rest of the board. The length of snipe increases with each pass.

If the outfeed table is set just a hair too high, boards come out convex. This can also happen if the infeed and outfeed tables tilt up and away from each other instead of being in parallel planes.

THE THICKNESS PLANER

The thickness planer is used to make one face of a board parallel to the other face. Whereas a jointer's cutterhead lies in the same plane as its tables, a planer's cutterhead is above the table and wood passes between them. The planer's infeed roller, outfeed roller and pressure bar force wood flat on the table as it passes through the machine.

The only way to get flat, straight lumber out of a planer is to feed in boards that already have one flat, straight face to put down against the table. A cupped board, fed through a planer, is flattened against the table by the rollers and pressure bar as it passes under the knives and then resumes its cupped shape as it exits the machine; it becomes a cupped board of uniform thickness. This is why surfaced boards from a lumberyard aren't ready for fine furniture. Lumberyards use only planers, not jointers, for surfacing wood—they make clean-faced boards of uniform thickness that aren't flat.

The standard-size planer used in small shops has knives 12 in. or 13 in. long. Larger shops may have planers with 20-in. or 30-in. knives. Thickness is set on some machines by raising or lowering the table. On other machines the cutterhead unit is moved up in down in relation to a stationary table. Some planers have variable-speed feed adjustments, which are very useful—they allow a slow feed on wood that threatens to tear out and a fast feed when you have to crank through a lot of board feet.

When a board is fed into a planer, the first thing that happens is that the ridged infeed roller grabs the wood, presses it down and pulls it along at a steady rate. Next, the board reaches the cutterhead, which, like that of a jointer, probably holds three straight steel knives spinning at incredibly high speed. The cutterhead skims off the thickness of wood it has been set for (ideally, never more than $\frac{1}{16}$ in. per pass) while the pressure bar keeps the wood from chattering. ("Chatter" occurs as wood vibrates under the impact of the knives, causing exaggerated parallel ridges across the board.) Then the smooth outfeed roller forces the wood even more firmly against the table and hastens it along.

Most planers have two rollers set into the table bed to minimize friction. The problem with these table rollers is that they can cause snipe (see pp. 44-45) if they are set too high by lifting the end of a board off the table while it is free of either the infeed or outfeed roller.

When milling a lot of rough wood down to approximate thickness I don't mind a little snipe, so I set the table rollers a hair above the surface to help the boards roll along. When I'm planing boards to final thickness and don't want any snipe, I lower the table rollers below the surface where they'll have no effect at all. I also keep my planer table waxed with paste wax or paraffin to minimize friction.

A thickness planer creates a second face parallel to the first.

USING THE THICKNESS PLANER

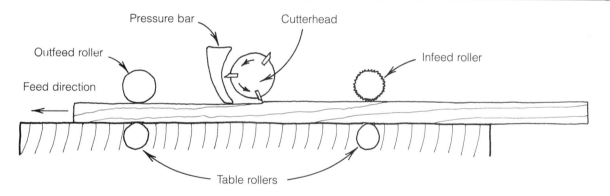

Another cause of snipe is a loose planer table that rocks as a board passes through. On a stationary-head planer, the gib screws that hold the table to the body of the machine should be so tight that the table just barely slides up and down for height adjustment.

One trick to avoid snipe is to feed a series of boards through the planer, butted together end to end. Only the front of the first board and the back of the last will have snipe.

Wood should be oriented in a thickness planer to cut with the grain, not against it. If grain runs both ways, take thin passes with sharp knives to minimize tearout.

THE DRILL PRESS

The drill press, which is used primarily to bore holes, provides the craftsman with more control than hand-held drills can. Most drill presses have stationary heads; their tables adjust for height and angle.

The main advantage of a drill press is that it can bore holes consistently square to the table (or at any angle up to 45°). The other virtue is a reliable depth-stop mechanism.

The speed at which a drill press turns is changed according to the material being bored and the diameter of the hole. Generally, metal should be bored at slower speeds than wood, and large holes should be bored at slower speeds than small ones. Some drill presses come with a variable-speed adjustment as easy as turning a handle; others require that you manually move drive belts onto different arrangements of pulleys in order to change speed.

Much of the time I place a piece of plywood or particleboard over the metal table of my drill press. Not only does this offer a larger work surface, it also keeps me from accidentally dulling drill bits on the metal table.

The drill press provides greater control than hand-held drills for boring holes.

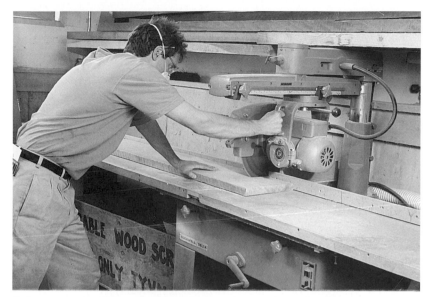

Side-extension tables make the radial-arm saw safer and easier to use.

THE RADIAL-ARM SAW

The radial-arm saw is essentially a large circular saw that is pulled along an overhead track. The arm can be raised or lowered to change the height of the blade relative to the table. The blade can also be angled to cut simple or compound miters. Saw size is specified by the diameter of the blade, which can range from 10 in. to 20 in. The most popular size radial-arm saw for small workshops takes a 12-in. diameter blade. Radial-arm-saw blades have their teeth set differently than blades used on table saws in order to diminish their tendency to "climb," or pull themselves through the wood.

Radial-arm saws can be used for crosscutting or ripping, but in my opinion ripping on this saw is dangerous and impractical—a bandsaw or table saw should be used instead. In my shop we use the radial-arm saw only for crosscutting rough lumber to approximate length at the start of the milling process (see p. 85). Radial-arm saws are considered too fickle for precise work, because they don't maintain accurate settings.

A good way to improve a radial-arm saw is to build side-extension tables, with fences, to support long boards. When crosscutting, always hold wood firmly against the fence so it can't move and catch the sawblade.

SAFETY TIPS FOR THE RADIAL-ARM SAW

1. Keep the blade sharp and free of pitch.

2. Never have your hand in the path of the blade.

3. Offer firm resistance against the travel of the blade while pulling it toward you; the blade will scream through anything in its way.

4. Never use the saw for ripping—it's just too dangerous.

THE LATHE

The lathe is made to spin wood so it can be shaped with a variety of steel tools and abrasives. The essential components of a lathe are the bed, headstock, tailstock, tool rest and motor. The headstock is stationary; the tailstock slides along the bed to accommodate spindle blanks of varying lengths.

By means of pulleys and a drive belt, the motor turns a shaft mounted horizontally through the headstock, which in turn drives the wood. Some lathes are variable speed; others require you to change speed by manually moving the drive belt onto different combinations of pulleys.

Two different types of turning can be done with a lathe: spindle turning and faceplate turning. Spindle turning is used to make chair rungs, legs, candlesticks, bed posts and stair balusters. Wood is suspended lengthwise between the headstock and the tailstock. The headstock is fitted with a spur center to drive the wood; the tailstock is fitted with a simple centering pin.

LATHE ANATOMY

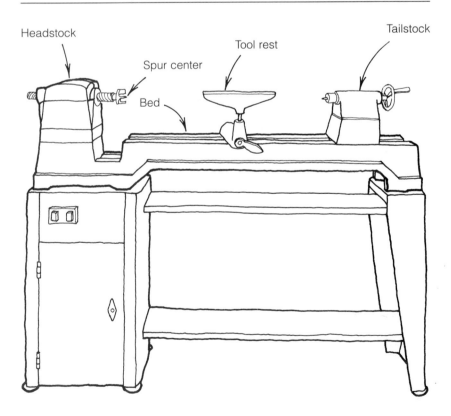

Headstock

Spur center

Tool rest

Tailstock

Bed

Faceplate turning is used to make bowls, plates and vases. A block of wood is screwed to a metal faceplate that attaches to the headstock. Large-diameter pieces can be turned by attaching the faceplate to the outside of the headstock and using a freestanding tool rest.

The hand tools used for spindle and faceplate turning include a variety of steel gouges, skew chisels, scrapers and parting tools, usually with long handles for greater control. They are always used with a tool rest, never freehand.

Lathes are specified according to the maximum length between the headstock and the tailstock, which is the length available for spindle turning, and the distance from the bed to the center of the drive shaft, which is the radius available for inboard faceplate turning.

The standard lathe that is found in many home and small professional woodshops will handle wood approximately 39 in. in length for spindle turning and about 16 in. in diameter for inboard faceplate turning.

The five projects presented in this book do not require use of the lathe. For further information on this basic woodworking machine, you might read *Creative Woodturning* by Dale Nish (Brigham Young University Press, 1975), *The Craftsman Woodturner* by Peter Child (Sterling Publishing Co., 1984) and *Turning Wood with Richard Raffan* (The Taunton Press, 1985).

THE CHOPSAW

Although it is not one of the essential tools in a furniture maker's shop, the chopsaw can be a time-saving auxiliary. The chopsaw, or miter saw, is a portable circular saw that pivots onto a slotted table. If adjusted accurately, it is good for cutting square or angled ends on small-dimensioned stock. My chopsaw, which has a 10-in. diameter blade, will make square cuts across wood up to 4¾ in. wide and 2¾ in. thick. Chopsaws are particularly useful to picture framers, who have to cut a lot of mitered corners.

As with the radial-arm saw, the utility of a chopsaw can be enhanced by building side-extension tables to support long boards. Always hold wood firmly against the fence. Don't cut pieces of wood less than 5 in. or 6 in. long; they can be difficult to hold securely without putting your fingers in jeopardy.

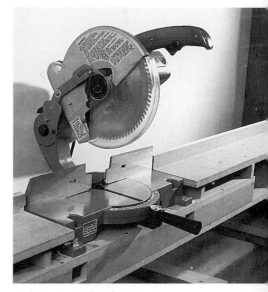

A chopsaw with side-extension tables is useful for making square or angled cuts on small stock.

THE ROUTER

Routers perform a wide variety of woodworking operations, including edge shaping, flush trimming, mortising, dovetailing, rabbeting, grooving and pattern-shaping. Although considered essential equipment for a modern woodshop, the router is not a substitute for hand skills. For example, router-cut dovetails can't match the variety of spacings and angles, or the delicacy, that make hand-cut dovetails so seductive to the eye.

Essentially, a router is a hand-held motor that spins a cutting bit at speeds up to 26,000 rpm. The motor is mounted in a base that can be adjusted to vary the depth of cut. There are fixed-speed and variable-speed routers. Variable speed is more pleasant to use, since at slower speeds the machine is quieter and less threatening.

A particularly useful accessory is a router table. A router is mounted upside-down beneath the table with the bit protruding upward through a hole. This arrangement allows you to move the wood against a stationary bit, rather than the other way around.

Many routers have a plunge feature that allows the bit to be lowered and raised through the base while the machine is running. Plunge routers are used for making mortises (see pp. 186-187) and for stopping and starting dado cuts.

Routers are specified according to collet size and horsepower. The collet (see the sidebar on the facing page) is the sleeve that receives the shank of a bit. Routers come with ¼-in., ⅜-in. or ½-in. collet capacities. Because bits with thicker shanks vibrate less, larger collet capacity is an advantage when working with large cutters.

Router motors range from ½ hp up to 3 hp. A commercial cabinet shop needs the brute strength of a 3-hp router, but furniture makers who use their router only occasionally can easily get by with less horsepower and, consequently, less noise.

Cutting bits for routers have edges of high-speed steel or carbide. Carbide is more expensive, but stays sharp so much longer that it's worth the cost. Edge-profile, flush-trim and rabbet bits generally have bearings attached that serve as fences.

Routers are used for a wide variety of woodworking operations, including edge shaping, flush trimming and mortising.

Router table with fence. A table-mounted router allows greater control than a hand-held router.

CHANGING ROUTER BITS

A router bit fits into a collet, which is held, in turn, within an opening on the end of the motor shaft. The collet is a metal sleeve with slits cut along its length. When a bit is installed, the pressure exerted by turning a threaded nut causes the collet to close tightly around the bit and simultaneously forces the collet into a friction fit within the motor-shaft opening. When you change bits, remove the collet and clean out any dust that may have collected around it. Otherwise, the trapped dust can burn off, reducing the friction that holds the collet in place and allowing the bit to pull loose.

ROUTER-BIT ASSEMBLY

 Router bit

Collet nut

 Collet

Motor shaft

THE SHAPER

The shaper is a larger, more powerful version of a router table and is used primarily for edge profiles, tongue-and-groove joinery, moldings, raised panels and pattern shaping. It is indispensable for commercial door and cabinet construction, but not at all necessary for making one-of-a-kind, fine furniture.

Many consider the shaper to be the most dangerous woodworking machine in the workshop. It can grab wood and draw a hand into the cutter quick as the flick of a hummingbird's wing. The use of shapers is not covered in this book.

THE GRINDER

Electric or hand-powered grinders are used in the sharpening process to restore hollow bevels to chisels and plane irons (see pp. 78-80). They are also good for reshaping screwdriver tips and performing other metal grinding tasks that come up from time to time. A grinder consists of one or two abrasive wheels mounted on a motor- or crank-driven shaft, with adjustable tool rests. Those used in woodshops commonly have 6-in., 7-in. or 8-in. diameter wheels.

I find electric grinders easier to use than hand-powered ones because they leave both hands free to hold the work. But because electric wheels spin faster, they are more likely to burn the steel. Once steel heats to the point where it turns blue or black, it loses its temper—its hardness—and won't keep a sharp edge for long.

My solution has been to buy an electric grinder with 7-in. wheels and a motor speed of 1,750 rpm, as opposed to the standard 6-in., 3,450-rpm model. The slower rotation reduces the amount of friction, and the larger wheel seems to give better results.

Hand-powered grinders usually have a single abrasive wheel turned by a crank. Their use requires more time and skill than do electric grinders, and purists love them. The strong points of hand grinders are that they are less likely to burn steel and they cost less. Used properly, both types of grinders yield comparable results.

An electric grinder is used for reshaping chisels, plane irons and other tools.

The surface of a grinding wheel can clog with steel or wear unevenly enough to chatter. Clogging is remedied with a steel dressing wheel. Chattering is remedied by reshaping the grinding wheel against a coarse carborundum stick.

Eye protection should be worn when using a grinder, even though many grinders are equipped with clear plastic shields to deflect the tiny bits of steel and abrasive that are thrown off. Also, grinding should only be done against the curve of the wheel. Grinding against the flat sides could cause a wheel to shatter, with disastrous results.

SANDERS

The two ways to work wood are to cut it or abrade it. Mastery of the hand skills involved in cutting (with saws, chisels, planes, scrapers, spokeshaves, and so on) requires more patience and practice than working with abrasives does; but cutting also provides more control and better results. I do very little sanding, and that is by hand. I don't care for the noise and dust generated by electric sanders.

My prejudices aside, sanders are very useful. They are commonly employed to flatten surfaces, fair curves, shape forms, round edges and smooth wood preparatory to finishing.

Sandpaper works by abrasion and leaves scratches behind. The finer the grit, the smaller the scratches. The smaller the scratches, the clearer the finished wood will appear. When I sand a tabletop with 150-grit paper, I sand until the entire surface is uniformly abraded and I have removed any scratches, tears or nicks deeper than those created by the sandpaper. Then I sand the entire surface with 220-grit paper to remove the scratches left by the 150-grit paper. If I were to keep going with finer and finer grits, I would eventually achieve a virtually polished surface disturbed only by the pores of the wood.

Sandpaper scratches blend in best when wood is sanded with the grain rather than across the grain. Of course, it doesn't matter which way you sand when you are simply trying to remove a lot of wood quickly. But when smoothing surfaces in preparation for finishing, always sand with the grain.

Sanders can be distinguished from one another by their motions: There are sanders that move a belt in a continuous loop, sanders that spin a disc, sanders that rotate a cylinder and sanders that move a sheet of sandpaper in an orbital motion. Brief descriptions follow.

BELT SANDERS

Hand-held belt sanders take continuous, replaceable belts of sandpaper. The most common size belts measure 3 in. or 4 in. in width and 20 in. or 24 in. in circumference. These sanders are used primarily to flatten and smooth large surfaces like tabletops. They remove wood so quickly that they are difficult to control and are prone to leave ridges and depressions.

Stationary belt sanders take belts 6 in. wide by 48 in. in circumference, and have an auxiliary table. They are used to flatten small surfaces and to round and smooth convex curves.

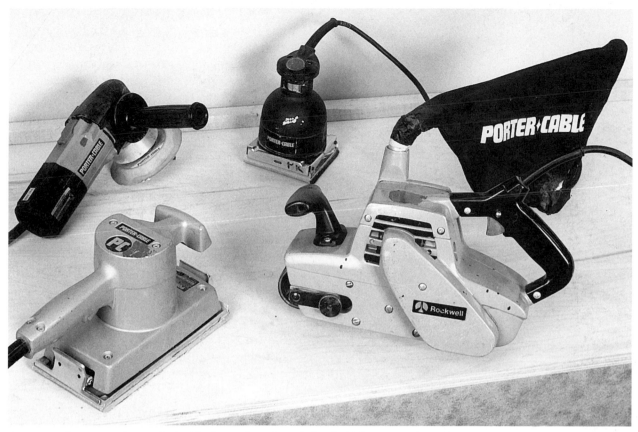

Common electric sanders include (clockwise from front left) a half-sheet orbital sander, a random orbital disc sander, a palm sander and a hand-held belt sander.

A stroke sander has a large belt, generally about 6 in. wide by 25 ft. in circumference, suspended between rollers above a table that slides from side to side. The spinning belt is stroked against a piece of wood with a hand-held platen from inside the loop. Stroke sanders are used in production shops for sanding large, flat surfaces.

"Time-savers" are stationary belt sanders that work like thickness planers. In place of a single cutterhead they have one, two or three belts that loop around rollers set above the table. Each consecutive belt spins a finer grit of sandpaper. Until recently, time-savers were found only in large production shops. Now smaller, less expensive versions are available.

DISC SANDERS

Hand-held disc sanders, also called grinders, have discs ranging from about 4 in. to 9 in. in diameter. They are used primarily for removing lots of wood quickly when sculpting forms. The circular motion of disc sanders makes it impossible to sand with the grain—they always leave cross-grain scratches.

Stationary units have discs ranging from 6 in. to 20 in. in diameter and a table. They are used for flattening small pieces of wood and the ends of butt joints, and to form and smooth convex curves. Wood should be sanded only on the side of the disc that spins down toward the table; the rising side will throw a piece of wood in your face.

DRUM SANDERS

Stationary drum sanders spin a horizontal or vertical cylindrical drum that is fitted with a cylindrical sanding sleeve. Drums come in a wide variety of diameters and lengths. Some are solid rubber, some are air-filled. They are used for shaping and smoothing concave and convex surfaces and for rounding edges.

ORBITAL SANDERS

The palm sander is probably the most useful sander for the craftsman making fine furniture. This small sander takes only a quarter-sheet of sandpaper. It is stroked in the direction of the grain and vibrates in small swirls, removing wood quite controllably. At the finer grits, the swirls become virtually invisible. Palm sanders are used for surface smoothing of flat and curved shapes.

Half-sheet orbital sanders, a larger form of the palm sander, are more useful on flat surfaces and less useful on curved ones.

RANDOM ORBITAL DISC SANDERS

Random orbital disc sanders unite the spin of a disc sander with the swirl of an orbital sander. In theory, they combine the fast wood removal of the former with the non-cross-grain-scratching of the latter. My own experience is that random orbital disc sanders are too jumpy and fast for sanding flat surfaces accurately. They are better for smoothing rounded edges.

BUYING MACHINERY

Buying woodworking machines is much like buying anything else—you get what you pay for. Don't try to save money by purchasing cheap equipment. Rickety frames, underpowered motors, and moving parts machined to poor tolerances add up to frustrating hours of work and bad results.

The best way to find out which machines are worth buying is to ask a professional woodworker who uses them all the time, rather than a salesperson. You'll be a lot more likely to get reliable information based on experience.

Even when buying a new machine made by a reputable · manufacturer, there are some things to look out for. Use a good straightedge to make sure tables are flat to within a few thousandths of a inch, especially on jointers and planers. Check to see that jointer tables are parallel to each other and that the fence isn't twisted along its length.

Look for runout in the spindles of boring machines, table saws and shapers. Runout, the degree to which a shaft spins eccentrically on its axis, should be only a few thousandths of an inch. A reputable machine dealer will measure runout for you.

Don't buy machines before you really need them. Remember, almost every woodworking operation can be done well with hand tools that cost considerably less. Purchase machinery only when you understand what is does and what you need it for, unless you are on a limitless budget.

Machines can't make you into a good craftsman; only practice and a willingness to master hand skills can do that. But machines can be a help and a time-saver for the craftsman who knows how they fit into the overall process.

INTRODUCTION TO
HAND TOOLS

The man-made devices that augment our bare hands in working wood can be divided into two classes: hand-driven tools and power-driven tools. Hand tools are to power tools what walking is to driving. Walking will get you just about anywhere. From urban back alleys to mountain meadows radiant with lupine and larkspur—you can walk as far off the "beaten path" as your heart desires. Walking immerses you in the environment; you trace the cragginess of pine bark with a fingertip, hear the splash of a trout, smell the air change as rain comes on.

Driving limits the choice of destination to places where roads already go; places accessible to anyone, anytime. You directly experience only the plastic, vinyl and glass of your car's interior. The natural environment passes behind the windshield as distant as a video on a television screen. Walking is about the journey, driving is about the destination.

Like walking, hand tools open an infinite range of form, surface texture and detail to the furniture maker. Hand work provides a depth of experience that power tools cannot. For example, when I smooth a tabletop with a jack plane instead of an electric sander, I hear the snick of the razor-sharp blade gliding through cherry, see the transparency of the shavings and feel the sole of the plane as it reveals each minute knoll and dip. With a sander, I experience only vibration, loud noise and dust.

The direct connection between a tool and the finely tuned nerves and muscles of your hand gives you direct experience of a piece of wood in all its quirky character. With power tools, one board seems no different than another.

Nothing happens except as you make it happen with hand tools. Your control is as complete as your skill. Work with hand tools is what British woodworker and author David Pye calls "the workmanship of risk"—the greater the individuality and character you strive for in making an object, the greater the risk of screwing up.

You might ask, "Does Korn ever get in a car, or does he walk everywhere?" Rest assured! When I lived in Colorado and wanted to see mountain wildflowers I didn't walk the 27 miles from my house to the trailhead; I drove. Then I climbed 2,000 vertical feet of narrow, rocky footpaths to high alpine meadows most people will never see. In the same way, I use a table saw, jointer, planer and bandsaw to rough out and thickness the parts of a stool. Then, with hand tools, I cut the joinery, fair the curves and smooth the surfaces.

What follows are descriptions of the basic hand tools that you need for furniture making.

THE WORKBENCH

The workbench is the single most important tool in the woodshop. It should be flat on top, strong enough to take a pounding and sturdy enough not to wobble.

A woodworking workbench generally incorporates a shoulder vise and a tail vise. The shoulder vise (see the top right photo on the facing page) holds wood against the edge of the bench. It is indispensable in hundreds of woodworking operations, such as marking and sawing joinery or hand planing an edge. The tail vise (see the bottom left photo on the facing page) mounts on the end of the workbench and lines up with a series of square holes evenly spaced along the top. Wood is held flat on the bench top between bench dogs inserted into the vise and the top. Because the bench dogs offer no obstruction, this setup is ideal for holding wood while face planing.

The functions of shoulder and tail vises are sometimes combined in a bench vise (see the bottom right photo on the facing page), which is essentially a shoulder vise that incorporates a dog. Mounted at the end of a workbench, it does the work of both vises.

The anvil vise commonly used by metalworkers is also extremely useful for woodworking, especially when fitted with wooden jaws to protect the work. Anvil vises hold work above the plane of the bench top. They can be mounted on the workbench or on a separate table.

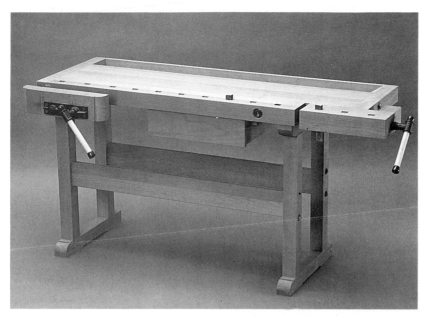

This European-style workbench, manufactured by Ulmia, incorporates a shoulder vise, a tail vise, a drawer and a tool tray.

A shoulder vise holds wood against the edge of the workbench.

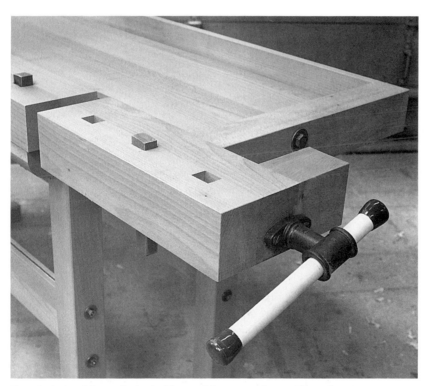

Bench dogs with a tail vise hold wood flat upon the workbench.

A bench vise (with auxiliary wooden jaws attached) combines the functions of the tail vise and the shoulder vise.

Whether your workbench is a $1,500 imported European beechwood affair or homemade out of particleboard, it deserves to be treated with the same respect as any other tool in your shop. For example, if you are going to drill or chisel through a board on the bench's surface, place scrap wood underneath to protect the bench top. If you use your bench for glue-ups, cover the surface with paper to catch any squeezed-out glue.

MEASURING TOOLS

The tradesman's traditional measuring tool, the folding wooden rule, has been largely supplanted over the past 40 years by the tape measure. I find both tools useful.

Tape measures are the handier choice when selecting and milling lumber. Since hardwood boards rarely come in lengths greater than 16 ft., a 16-ft. tape is sufficient. For the more exacting work of marking joinery and fitting, I prefer a **folding rule.** It is easier to handle, doesn't flex and stays where I lay it. One folding rule—a Lufkin Red-end Carpenter's Rule with extension slide—is superior to all the rest. Made from sturdy boxwood, the Lufkin rule is not as likely to break as inferior models. The extension is handy for taking inside measurements and for checking hole depths.

SQUARES, STRAIGHTEDGES AND T-BEVELS

Squares are used to make sure things are at right angles to one another. In a woodshop, these things might be the edge of a board, the shoulder of a tenon, the fence on a jointer, the end of a chisel, the sides of a drawer, the leg of a chair, and so on.

Square is an abstract term. Looked at closely enough, nothing is truly square; some things just approach the ideal more than others. A furniture maker's square should be square within the tolerances of woodworking, which are more stringent than a house framer's, but less precise than a machinist's. There are three types of square that I find useful: try squares, engineer's squares and framing squares.

Try squares are the most commonly used squares among furniture makers. They have blades of brass or steel (generally from 6 in. to 12 in. long) set in a thicker wood or metal stock. If the stock is wood, it should be faced with metal to ensure long-term accuracy.

The reliability of try squares can vary sharply, even among those made by the same manufacturer. I once made the mistake of ordering inexpensive try squares by mail. Two out of three were so far off that I threw them in the trash barrel. The only way to buy a square is to pick it out yourself or order it from one of the few makers who guarantee accuracy to extremely close tolerances. If you are selecting your own try square, check it against one of the engineer's squares the tool store is likely to have on hand.

Engineer's squares are similar in design to try squares, but made entirely of steel. Blade lengths start at about 2 in. These squares are more reliable than try squares, probably because engineers are a more demanding lot than woodworkers. Engineer's squares can be used interchangeably with try squares in a woodshop.

Framing squares are made for house building. They have two large blades that form a right angle. One blade is 2 in. wide by 24 in. long; the other is 1½ in. by 18 in. long. Framing squares are not expected to be as precise as try squares or engineer's squares. I find them useful when building large cabinets or doing carpentry.

Whether made of metal, wood or plastic, a **straightedge** comes in handy for such things as checking the flatness of boards and drawing straight lines. I keep 24-in. and 48-in. steel rules hanging by my tool cabinet. When I need a longer straightedge I use an 8-ft. scrap of medium-density fiberboard (MDF).

A flexible metal straightedge is also useful for drawing smooth curves. When making full-scale drawings of curved parts, I often bend a metal rule between my hands and, if no one is there to help, trace the curve with a pencil held between my teeth.

The **sliding T-bevel** is used to transfer and mark angles. Metal-bodied T-bevels generally have more reliably straight shoulders than do wooden ones. Some poorly designed T-bevels use wing nuts instead of thumbscrews as locking devices. Unfortunately, a wing nut can hold the stock off the work in certain positions.

TRY SQUARE

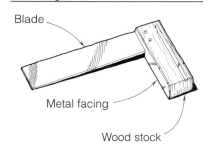

Blade

Metal facing

Wood stock

SLIDING T-BEVEL

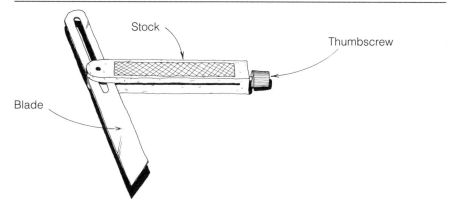

Stock

Thumbscrew

Blade

MARKING TOOLS

Every workshop seems to be haunted by a pencil-hoarding goblin. One minute a pencil is behind your ear, the next it has disappeared without a trace.

Ordinary, school-type **pencils** are useful for marking wood in order to keep track of jointed surfaces and which pieces fit together. Another type of pencil that is particularly useful for woodworking is the **lead holder** made for drafting. Lead holders are ideal for marking out joints, as well as for drafting and drawing, because they take a much finer point than a school pencil, and a precise line can be crucial to accurate joinery.

Leads come in a range of hardness from 6B (softest) to 6H (hardest). Harder lead makes a fainter line, but holds a point longer. I use an H or 2H lead to mark out joinery.

Knives are indispensable in a woodshop for tasks as varied as marking tenon shoulders and cutting cardboard templates. I've seen woodworkers use every kind of knife, from a Boy Scout penknife to a reground file. My preference is a common utility knife with replaceable blades that can be bought at any hardware store.

Awls are sharp, pointed instruments with a variety of uses. They differ in the fineness of their points and the thickness of their shafts. A fine-pointed awl is useful for marking out joinery and scribing lines (though I find a pencil line easier to read on all but dark woods). A thick-shanked, broad-pointed awl (see the drawing at left) is good for making pilot holes in wood prior to drilling. The dimple it leaves when tapped with a mallet forms an exact starting point for a drill bit.

AWL

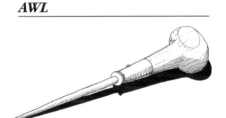

MORTISING GAUGE

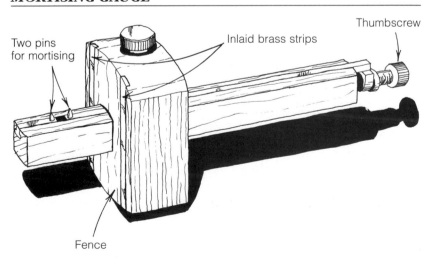

Two pins for mortising

Inlaid brass strips

Thumbscrew

Fence

Marking and mortising gauges are used to lay out joinery. A **marking gauge** incorporates a single pin and an adjustable fence for scribing a single line parallel to an edge. A **mortising gauge** is similar, except that it has two pins that can be adjusted in relation to one another and scribes a double line.

Marking and mortising gauges can be bought as separate tools or put together in a **combination gauge.** I prefer to have them separate for two reasons. First, some projects require both single and double lines. Changing the settings back and forth on a combination gauge takes time and decreases accuracy. Second, when I use the combination tool I invariably stab my thumb on the pin that isn't in use.

For many applications, the pin on a marking gauge should be filed thin so it will slice across wood fibers cleanly like a knife, rather than tear fibers like an awl. A thin pin is particularly important for laying out the shoulders of dovetails.

When you are purchasing a marking, mortising or combination gauge, make sure that the fence is flat. Inlaid brass strips make a fence more durable.

SAWS

The projects in this book call for the furniture maker's most commonly used saws—a backsaw, a coping saw and perhaps a handsaw.

Backsaw describes a family of saws whose blades are stiffened with metal spines. Backsaws, also known as dovetail saws, vary in blade thickness, width and length, and in tooth size and tooth set. Those with thin blades and tiny teeth are for fine work; those with thick blades and coarser teeth cut relatively roughly and rapidly.

BACKSAW

The saw I use for cutting joinery is an inexpensive, small backsaw with a blade 10 in. long by 1⅝ in. wide. With 21 tiny teeth per inch, it leaves a very thin kerf. I get excellent control and accuracy with this saw, but I've seen other furniture makers do just as well with traditional English backsaws that have wider blades or with Japanese saws that cut on the pull stroke.

A **coping saw** cuts curves and can also cut interior shapes out of a board. When making dovetails, I use a coping saw to remove the waste wood between the pins or the tails.

COPING SAW

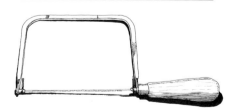

To saw an interior shape, drill a hole through the wood to be removed, take the coping saw apart, stick the blade through the hole and reassemble the saw around the blade. A coping saw cannot cut farther in from the wood's edge than the distance between the sawblade and the saw frame. Coping-saw blades come in packages of five or more—when one breaks or gets dull you simply install another.

HANDSAW

Handsaws have more or less been bypassed by the age of machinery. They have become a standby for those times when power tools are not available or won't work. For example, because I can't trust the lumberyard to have a sharp saw on hand, I take a handsaw along in case I need to cut a board to fit in my vehicle. I also use a handsaw to crosscut boards that are too thick for my power saws to handle.

The teeth of handsaws are set (angled) for either crosscutting or ripping. A saw with more teeth per inch leaves a smoother surface but cuts more slowly. A saw is sharpened by having its teeth filed and their angles reset. You can do this in your own workshop, but I feel that sending my handsaws (as well as my circular-saw blades, jointer and planer knives, and router bits) out to be professionally sharpened is a better use of my time.

DRILLS

HAND DRILLS

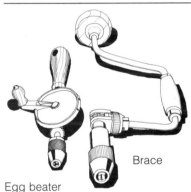

Brace

Egg beater

Hand-powered drills have, for the most part, been replaced in the workshop by electric drills. There are still times, however, when a hand drill is preferable: to drill in a tight space; for increased control; or for the simple pleasure of using a quieter, lighter tool. Two types of hand drill are the egg beater and the brace.

DRILL BITS
The drill bits found in a woodshop include twist drills, brad-point bits, Forstner bits and spade bits. Each has distinct advantages and limitations.

Twist drills will make holes in wood, metal, plastic and just about any other material. They are a necessary item for the woodworker because of their versatility and their great range of closely graduated diameters (from ¹⁄₁₆ in. to 1 in. by sixty-fourths). The disadvantages of twist drills for furniture making are twofold: they are difficult to center perfectly and tend to walk before establishing a location, and they often drill holes that are slightly elliptical.

Brad-point bits have center spurs that engage wood before the cutting edge makes contact, so holes are perfectly round and exactly placed. Commonly available in sizes from ⅛ in. to ½ in. by sixteenths, and from ½ in. to 1 in. by eighths, brad points are generally the best bits for woodworking, though they are useless for drilling metal.

In those rare situations where a hole goes so deep that the protruding spur of a brad point would poke through to the other side, a **Forstner bit** can be used. The center spurs of Forstner bits are flush with the cutters. They aren't self-centering the way brad-point bits are,

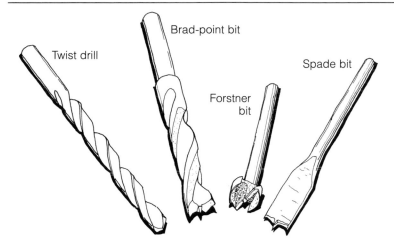

but they make extremely clean, flat-bottomed holes. Because Forstner bits are more expensive than brad points, cut more slowly and heat up faster, I rarely use them.

In my experience, **spade bits** are of little use for woodworking. Why they are so widely sold in hardware stores and lumberyards is a mystery to me. They create oval-shaped, inaccurate holes, tear out surfaces and immediately dull on hardwoods.

CHISELS

The chopping and paring abilities of chisels make them useful in so many ways that scarcely a day goes by that the furniture maker doesn't use one. They are essential to hand cutting and fitting of joinery, especially mortise-and-tenon joints and dovetails.

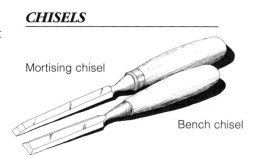

There are two families of chisels: those with beveled edges (bench and paring chisels) and those with square edges (mortising chisels). **Bench chisels** are durably made to take on any job. **Paring chisels** are lighter in construction and meant only for paring under hand control rather than for chopping under a mallet. **Mortising chisels** are specialized for the heavy work of chopping mortises.

The first set of chisels a furniture maker needs are bench chisels in widths of ¼ in., ⁵⁄₁₆ in., ⅜ in., ½ in., ¾ in., 1 in. and 1¼ in. I also have a few mortising chisels (¼ in., ⁵⁄₁₆ in., ⅜ in. and ½ in.), but for many years I got by perfectly well without them. I find no need for paring chisels in my workshop.

Chisels vary in worth according to the steel in their blades and the durability of their handles. The quality and temper of the steel are of first importance. Steel that is either too soft or too brittle won't hold a sharp edge. Inexpensive chisels sometimes have thin blades that tend to bend from use or warp from the heat of grinding.

A chisel handle that is badly made or poorly attached won't hold up under serious use. Wooden handles are fine for the light work of paring, but I prefer durable plastic handles that will stand up to a mallet.

Leave your chisels sharp at the end of each day's work. It is a great pleasure to reach into your tool cabinet and pull out a chisel sharp enough to shave hair, rather than interrupt the flow of work with a dull blade. Detailed instructions for sharpening chisels are given on pp. 78-81.

MALLETS

WOODEN MALLETS

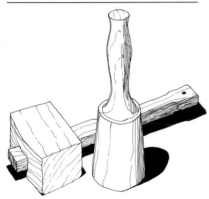

Wooden mallets, metal hammers and rubber mallets are the three striking implements generally found in a woodshop. Of the three, wooden mallets are best for driving chisels. They deliver firm impact with minimum damage to the chisel handle. A metal hammer would be too destructive, and the impact of a rubber mallet is too cushioned to be effective.

Wooden mallets either have their heads mounted at right angles to a shaft or are cylindrical turnings. I prefer a cylindrical mallet—it has better balance, and is ready to strike however I pick it up. Mallets come in a variety of weights. The right weight for you is whatever you find effective and comfortable.

Rubber mallets are best for fitting joints or knocking furniture together during glue-ups. They are the least likely to dent wood. If glue has begun to set and a joint gets stubborn, I switch to a hammer for greater impact, but interpose a piece of scrap wood to avoid dents.

PLANES

The basic planes for furniture making are bench planes and block planes, which are used to flatten and smooth wood surfaces. Scrub planes are also useful in the initial stages of flattening a board. A wide variety of specialty planes exists for rabbeting, molding edges and forming convex and concave surfaces, among other things.

Bench planes generally come in lengths from 9 in. to 24 in. The longer the plane, the flatter the surface it leaves. Where a straight, square edge is needed for gluing one board to another, you might use a 24-in. jointer plane. A 9-in. smoothing plane, on the other hand, would be used to clean small defects from an already flattened surface. If I could have only one plane for all-around use, it would be a 14-in. jack plane.

Some bench planes come with corrugated soles to decrease friction. Smooth soles are fine, though, as long as you occasionally wax them with paraffin.

Block planes are shorter than bench planes, usually about 6 in. long. Their blades are set at a lower angle to minimize tearout when planing end grain. I use a block plane to flatten end-grain surfaces, make dovetails and through tenons flush after glue-up, chamfer edges and smooth convex surfaces.

Scrub planes are flat-bottomed wood planes with convex cutting edges. They are moved across or diagonal to the grain to flatten rough lumber quickly. Pushed along the grain, scrub planes can make nasty tearouts.

Rabbet planes are used primarily to make dadoes and rabbets and to clean up the shoulders and cheeks of tenons. The sides of a rabbet plane are machined square to the sole, and the blade is the full width of the body. Some rabbet planes are bullnosed—the front can be removed to allow the blade into corners.

Molding planes are rarely used anymore; they have been largely replaced by routers. I don't own a single one, but then I rarely desire a fancy molded edge on my furniture.

Until the 19th century, all planes were wood-bodied, with wooden wedges to hold the irons in place. Depth of cut and blade angle were adjusted by tapping the iron with a hammer. Today, most commercially available planes are made of metal, with mechanical blade adjustments. I use metal-bodied planes, but there are some furniture makers who feel that wooden planes are more sensitive instruments. Wooden planes are available commercially, but some aficionados prefer to make their own.

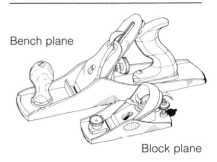

PLANES

Bench plane

Block plane

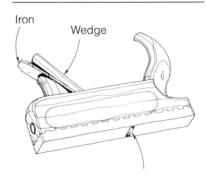

SCRUB PLANE

Iron

Wedge

Convex cutting edge

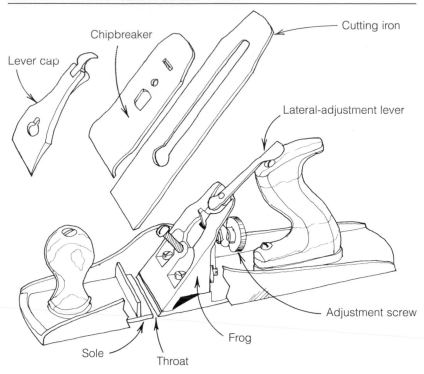

The key to using any plane is in tuning it up. Bench and block planes should have flat soles, and very few come that way from the manufacturer. Whenever you get a new plane, plan to spend a few hours rubbing the bottom flat. (One method for flattening the plane's sole is given on p. 80.)

The second major requirement of a well-tuned plane is that the blade be razor sharp, with the bevel ground to about 25°. (Detailed instructions for sharpening plane blades are given on pp. 78-81.) If you ever wonder whether the blade in a particular plane should be inserted bevel up or bevel down, remember that manufacturers want their names to be visible at all times. The side on which the name is engraved faces up!

The size of the throat—the space where shavings pass between the blade and the sole—should be experimented with for optimum performance. Throat size is controlled on a metal bench plane by sliding the frog forward or back. Generally, throat size is increased to take coarser shavings when flattening rough boards, and decreased to take fine shavings and reduce tearout during final smoothing.

The chipbreaker should be set just behind the cutting edge of the blade—about $\frac{1}{32}$ in. to $\frac{1}{16}$ in. This part of the plane breaks shavings to keep them from tearing out ahead of the cutting iron. It also stiffens the cutting iron and prevents it from chattering.

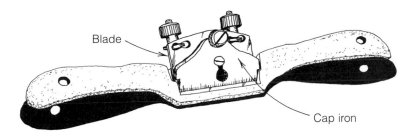

Blade

Cap iron

SPOKESHAVES

A spokeshave is a type of plane used primarily to round edges, make spindles and fair concave curves. The short sole of a spokeshave is mounted between two handles. The blade is generally held in place with a cap iron. Spokeshaves can be used with either a pulling or a pushing motion.

Spokeshaves are made with flat, convex or concave soles. For general use, a flat sole is sufficient.

SCRAPERS AND BURNISHERS

When I was a 22-year-old, inexperienced house carpenter, I went to Spain. Under a makeshift awning at a hillside flea market, an old man who was selling his woodworking tools drew sinuous shavings from a board with only a thin, flat piece of metal. I imagined I was witnessing a secret of ancient craftsmanship that he would take to his grave. But I was too shy to ask questions, so it was several more years before I learned that his magic was a common hand scraper.

A **hand scraper** is a thin, flat piece of soft steel, about 3 in. wide and 6 in. long. When the edge is burnished—stroked with a harder piece of steel—it rolls over into a barely perceptible, wood-cutting hook. A properly sharpened hand scraper takes shavings without any tearout.

Scrapers are used to smooth surfaces prior to sanding and finishing. Not all scrapers are straight-edged. Curved scrapers are used to smooth forms that are curved in section. Scrapers can be cut and filed to special shapes for individual jobs, such as beading an edge.

Although the hand scraper is the simplest tool in the woodshop, it is, paradoxically, the most difficult to master. Instructions are given on pp. 150-151.

A **cabinet scraper** is a combination of hand scraper and spokeshave. A scraper blade projects through a sole between two handles. A cabinet scraper keeps a surface fairly flat, whereas a hand scraper is more likely to create small hollows. However, I find a hand scraper to be the more versatile, useful tool and rarely have recourse to a cabinet scraper.

Burnishers are smooth rods of hard steel used to put an edge on a scraper. They can be round, oval or triangular in section. A highly polished burnisher creates a smoother edge on the scraper, which in turn leaves the scraped wood smoother. The shank of a Phillips-head screwdriver often works well as a burnisher.

FILES AND RASPS

Wood files and rasps are used primarily to abrade edges and curves in wood. Files are lengths of hard steel whose surfaces have been scored in regular patterns. The depth of the scoring and the nature of the pattern determine the degree of abrasiveness. Files come in a variety of shapes including flat, half-round (flat on one side and rounded on the other), round and triangular. A good, all-purpose file for woodworking is a 10-in. half-round "wood" or "cabinet" file. For flattening scrapers and other metal filing tasks, an 8-in. mill bastard file is a handy addition to the woodshop.

Rasps are lengths of hard steel on which small teeth have been raised. Less expensive rasps have machined-raised teeth in regular patterns. They leave a rougher surface than the more expensive cabinetmaker's rasps, whose teeth are hand-raised in random patterns. My first choice of rasp would be the coarsest cabinetmaker's rasp available, which is called a "second cut." It will remove wood quickly, but relatively cleanly.

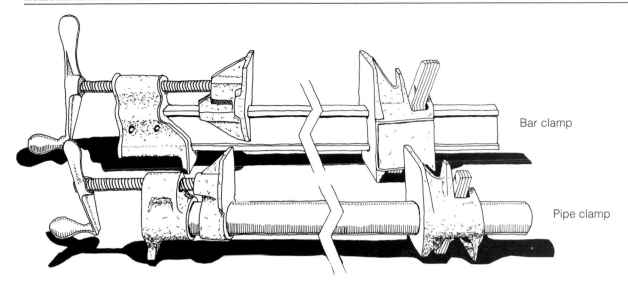

Bar clamp

Pipe clamp

CLAMPS

Clamps are used to squeeze pieces of wood together, particularly during assembly and gluing. The major varieties are bar clamps, pipe clamps, quick-action clamps, C-clamps, hand screws, band clamps and spring clamps.

A **bar clamp** consists of two jaws mounted on a length of steel bar, usually I-shaped in section. One jaw is fixed at the head of the bar and tightens on the work by means of a vise-thread and handle. The other jaw slides along the bar to whatever fixed position is desirable. A **pipe clamp** is similar except that it substitutes pipe for I-bar and is consequently less rigid. Bar and pipe clamps are best suited for assembling wide surfaces, such as tabletops, and for putting together large carcases.

Quick-action clamps have a fixed jaw at one end of a flat steel bar. A second jaw, which incorporates a vise-thread and handle, slides on the bar to fix in any position. Quick-action clamps come in a range of sizes from 6-in. to 36-in. maximum open span between the jaws.

Besides length, the two variables in quick-action clamps are throat depth and bar size. Throat depth (the distance from the tip of the jaws to the bar) limits the distance the clamp will reach in from the edge of a board. Bar size relates to strength—a clamp with a thicker bar exerts more pressure with less flex.

Quick-action clamp

C-clamp

Hand screw

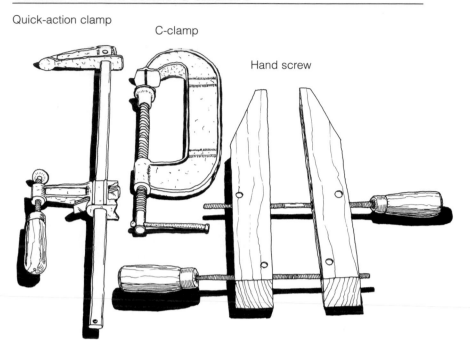

Quick-action clamps are the workhorse among clamps. They are constantly in use for holding work on a bench, improvising fences on machinery, clamping bent laminations, assembling chairs and small carcases, and performing countless other tasks.

C-clamps have a C-shaped metal body with a vise-thread and handle entering at one end. Like other clamps, they come in a wide variety of lengths, throat depths and bar thicknesses. C-clamps can be used interchangeably with quick-action clamps, though in many situations they are more cumbersome.

Hand screws have wooden jaws that are moved together or apart by means of wooden vise-threads. I find them awkward to use compared to metal clamps. One advantage of hand screws is that their wooden jaws are less likely than metal to damage the work, but this inequality is easily addressed by inserting pieces of scrap wood under metal jaws.

A **band clamp** is a loop of strong, woven material, such as nylon, that begins and ends at a tightening device that draws the loop smaller. Band clamps can exert tremendous pressure, and are particularly useful for clamping together forms whose rounded shapes or parts don't work well with ordinary clamps.

Spring clamps do not exert the degree of pressure that other clamps do. They are useful for small repairs and as extra hands for holding things in place.

BUYING HAND TOOLS

Good tools contribute to good craftsmanship. Cheap tools are a waste of money—they compromise the quality of your work and the pleasure you take in it. I've had students throw thin-bladed chisels into the trash barrel on the second day of class.

The best tools are not necessarily the most expensive ones available. Rosewood and brass may be seductive, but what you really want are tools that are well designed for the task at hand, durably constructed and made to close tolerances.

Finding a retail outlet for quality hand tools can be difficult in many places. Fortunately, there are several reliable, reasonably priced mail-order companies that offer good selections. Two that I particularly recommend are Woodcraft in Parkersburg, West Virginia, and Woodworkers Supply in Albuquerque, New Mexico. For a list of mail-order suppliers' addresses and phone numbers, see p. 196.

THE WORKING ENVIRONMENT

A good shop environment contributes to the quality and pleasure of your work. Good lighting, and plenty of it, is essential. Standard fluorescent bulbs cast a generalized light that minimizes shadows and makes marking and cutting easier. Incandescent bulbs are less tiring to the eyes over a long day. New technologies are being developed that may combine the virtues of both, but I have yet to try them.

A window, in addition to light, provides connection with the world outside. Life in the workshop joins the cycles of sun and weather. A workshop without a window can feel like a prison cell.

Order and cleanliness increase efficiency and safety. It has always been my habit to put tools away and sweep up at the end of each day's work. Not only does this allow me to find things quickly when I need them and to work without obstruction—I also feel a greater sense of excitement when I walk into a clean shop first thing in the morning.

Rare is the woodworker who feels that his or her shop is large enough. For many years I worked in one- and two-car garages. My planer was on wheels so I could roll it out of the way. When I eventually moved into a 1,200-sq. ft. shop, I was so ecstatic that I didn't mind the absence of heat over the first winter. After several years, however, even 1,200 ft. began to feel cramped.

In the long run, the size of the shop is not really important. What counts is the enjoyment you get from working in it. Wherever you work, think of your shop as a valuable tool. Take care to make it a light, pleasant, orderly environment, and it will repay you handsomely.

A perfectly ground chisel reflects light evenly across the bevel.

Magnification reveals the serrated edge left by the grinding wheel. (Chisel photos by Susan Kahn.)

GRINDING AND SHARPENING

Good craftsmanship not only requires decent tools, it also demands that those tools be properly maintained. Sharp chisels and plane blades are essential. Unfortunately, many woodworkers begrudge the time sharpening takes, probably because they aren't very good at it. Once you have the right equipment and know how to use it, though, sharpening becomes second nature.

Two tools are used in the sharpening process: a grinding wheel and sharpening stones. The grinding wheel shapes and maintains the bevel at the business end of the blade. The stones hone the leading edge of the bevel to ultimate sharpness. If you are just learning to grind and sharpen, it is easier to practice on a wide chisel. Narrow chisels are more likely to gouge the surface of a sharpening stone.

GRINDING

Electric grinders are usually mounted with two carborundum wheels, one medium grit and one coarse grit. Medium grit is best for general shop work.

Sometimes a buffing wheel is substituted for one of the carborundum wheels for the purpose of honing chisels and plane blades. This is a mistake. The tiny bevel created by a buffing wheel breaks a cardinal rule of sharpening, which is to keep the back of the blade perfectly flat. A flat-backed blade has two advantages. First, it makes perfect sharpening quicker and easier. Second, a flat-backed blade cuts better, especially on a chisel, where it can serve as a guide to flatness while paring. Buffing wheels are more appropriate for sharpening carving tools than for furniture-making tools.

How to grind a bevel

The goal of grinding is to create a uniform hollow bevel across the edge of the blade. The hollow is the concave surface left by the circumference of the grinding wheel. A blade requires grinding when it is nicked or when its bevel becomes flat from repeated honing on stones.

Some grinders have horizontally mounted wheels that are designed to create a flat bevel. But a flat bevel is a disadvantage when it comes time to hone the blade on stones. If the bevel angle is to be maintained, more steel has to be removed to affect the cutting edge sufficiently (see the drawing on p. 81).

To the unpracticed eye, a perfectly ground blade looks as though it has a straight, sharp edge. Examined under a magnifying glass, however, the edge reveals itself to be unevenly serrated. The ideal of a perfect edge can never be attained, but the more closely it is approximated, the sharper a blade will be. After grinding, sharpening stones are employed to create ever-finer serrated edges.

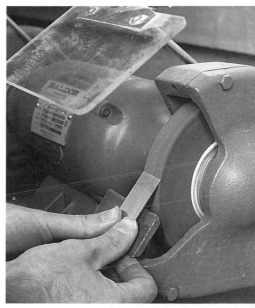

To grind a bevel, hold the blade flat on the tool rest with your thumbs.

Before you begin grinding, sight between the blade and the grinding wheel to make sure the tool rest is adjusted to the correct angle.

The steps involved in grinding are as follows:

1. Adjust the grinder's tool rest. With the blade held flat on the rest, the bevel should meet the grinding wheel at the desired angle. The bevels of chisels and plane irons are usually ground to 25°.
2. Turn the grinder on and hold the blade just shy of the spinning wheel. The hand position that works best for me entails holding the blade flat on the tool rest with my thumbs and using the edges of my forefingers as guides along the lower lip of the rest.
3. With your hands in position and the blade held flat on the tool rest, slide the blade up until it just makes contact with the wheel.
4. Move the blade from side to side, keeping it flat on the tool rest and square to the face of the grinding wheel. The side-to-side movement helps to grind an even bevel and wears the wheel uniformly. (Grinding a curved blade, such as that of a scrub plane, involves moving the blade in an arcing motion.)

Never force a blade against the wheel. Heat is inevitable, but excessive pressure makes a blade heat up faster than necessary. The thin steel at the cutting edge heats very quickly once it comes in contact with the wheel. To avoid overheating the steel, dip it frequently in water.

Grinding takes practice. I find that, within a week, any student who is determined has mastered the art of sharpening, though usually not without doing horrendous things to innocent chisels and plane irons along the way. Fortunately, grinding is like riding a bicycle—once you have the skill, you never lose it.

SHARPENING STONES

After a blade has been ground to a hollow bevel, it can be honed on stones a number of times before the hollow disappears enough to warrant regrinding.

Sharpening stones are either man-made or natural, and are used with either oil or water as a lubricant to prevent clogging. Natural oilstones are called, in order of increasing fineness, washita, soft arkansas, hard arkansas and black arkansas. They are lubricated with oil thinned with kerosene, and are the traditional choice of American craftsmen. Coarser man-made oilstones, called crystolon and India, are often used in combination with natural stones.

Man-made, ceramic Japanese waterstones are a recent introduction to Western woodworkers. Japanese waterstones cut faster than natural stones and are more easily kept flat. Best of all, they are lubricated with water, which eliminates oil on tools, fingers, rags and wood. Switching from oilstones to waterstones was the best thing that ever happened in my sharpening life.

Flattening the back

The first rule of sharpening is that the back side of the blade must stay perfectly flat. (It is all right to leave small hollows in the back of a blade, as long as they do not occur along the cutting edge or the sides.)

New chisels and plane irons almost always need to have their backs flattened, as do the soles of new planes. The process can take hours, but is well worth it. Lay a sheet of 220-grit wet/dry sandpaper or 220-grit carborundum mesh paper on a flat surface such as a jointer table or a piece of plate glass. Rub the back of the blade flat on the paper, using thin oil or water as a lubricant. (Don't use water when working on a machine table, or it will rust.)

When the back of the blade is uniformly abraded, switch from sandpaper to a medium-grit sharpening stone, such as a 1000-grit waterstone or a soft arkansas. Lubricate the surface of the stone with oil or water, whichever it takes. When the stone has uniformly polished the back, switch to a fine stone, such as a 6000-grit waterstone or a hard arkansas, and repeat.

By the time you are finished, the back of the blade will be like a mirror. From then on, it should make contact only with your finest sharpening stone and never need flattening again.

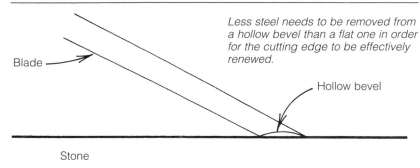

Blade

Less steel needs to be removed from a hollow bevel than a flat one in order for the cutting edge to be effectively renewed.

Hollow bevel

Stone

When honing on stones, keep your arms rigid and rock from the knees to maintain the blade at a constant angle.

Honing on stones

Whether a blade is newly ground or simply needs re-honing, the process of sharpening on stones is the same:

1. Place the bevel flat on a medium-grit stone such as a 1000-grit waterstone or a soft arkansas. The front and back ridges of the hollow grind will be in contact with the stone.
2. Push the blade forward with a light downward pressure. Bring the blade back with no downward pressure at all. (Honing a curved blade involves pushing it forward in a sweeping arc.)
3. To keep the blade at a constant angle, move your entire body, not just your arms.
4. Use a modified figure-eight motion to wear the surface of the stone evenly.
5. Hone until the cutting edge has been affected all the way across. You can gauge this by the appearance of the steel, which will reflect light differently where it is freshly honed. You can also feel the back of the blade for the wire edge of steel that has been pushed over from the bevel side.

Pull the wire edge off the back of the chisel on a fine stone.

At this point, switch to a fine stone. With waterstones I jump to 6000 grit. With oilstones you might go to a hard arkansas. Lay the back of the blade flat on the fine stone and pull off the wire edge.

Repeat steps 1 through 5 on the fine stone. Then pull the wire edge off again. A few more strokes on the bevel side, another pull-off on the back, and soon there will be no discernible wire edge. The blade will be sharp enough to shave with. When I am busy in my shop, the backs of my hands become bald from testing chisels for sharpness. A cutting edge this sharp not only makes planing, paring and chopping a pleasure, but is also intrinsic to quality craftsmanship.

PROJECT 1:

MILLING
A BOARD
FOUR-SQUARE

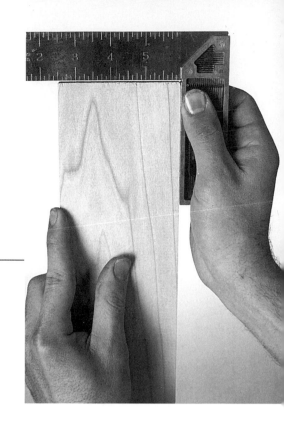

This chapter presents the first in a series of exercises that build upon one another sequentially. If you are already competent at the machine milling process and hand planing, you might read this chapter as a review. If this information is new to you or you are still learning, practice milling a board four-square before going on to the more complex projects that follow.

"Milling a board four-square" means cutting a piece of lumber to thickness, width and length, and making it straight, flat and square-edged in the process. The tools most commonly used in this operation are the jointer, the thickness planer and the table saw. This chapter also explores the use of the bandsaw, the radial-arm saw, handsaws and hand planes.

The project may seem simple, but it incorporates many basic understandings. These include the meaning of "square," how to measure, and the safe use of machinery. Where instructions are given to use a particular machine, please review the general safety information on p. 35, as well as the individual section on that machine in the same chapter.

HOW TO MILL
FOUR-SQUARE STOCK

Our goal is to end up with a piece of wood ¾ in. thick by 3½ in. wide by 24 in. long. The board you start with should be larger in each dimension. Depending on how warped, bowed or cupped the initial board is, you can expect to lose at least ⅛ in. of thickness and ¼ in. of width in the milling process.

In class, I usually start students with a piece of roughsawn 4/4 poplar about 4 in. wide and 25 in. long. You can use any type of hardwood, but poplar is inexpensive and easy to work with.

The steps in the milling process are as follows (note that steps 4 and 5 are often reversed):

1. CUT A LONG BOARD TO APPROXIMATE LENGTH.

2. RIP TO APPROXIMATE WIDTH.

3. FLATTEN ONE FACE.

4. SQUARE ONE EDGE TO THE FLAT FACE.

5. PLANE THE SECOND FACE PARALLEL TO THE FIRST.

6. RIP THE BOARD TO FINISHED WIDTH.

7. CUT ONE END SQUARE.

8. CUT THE OTHER END SQUARE AND TO LENGTH.

STEP 1. **CUT TO APPROXIMATE LENGTH.**

If you start with a long board, the first thing to do is cut off a section to approximate length, using either a crosscut handsaw or a radial-arm saw. Begin by examining the end of the board for splits and checks. If there are any, square a pencil line across the board where the cracks end.

To use a square:

If you are using a try square, hold its stock parallel to and firmly against the edge of the board, as shown in the photo at right. Two common mistakes are holding the square by the blade, which allows the stock to rock out of alignment with the edge, and holding the square with the blade perpendicular to the surface of the board rather than flat upon it.

To use a handsaw:

Make sure the board is well supported on a workbench or sawhorses. Low sawhorses make it easier to put your weight behind the saw. Get a foot or a clamp on the board so it won't move. Use a diagonal, downward sawing motion at the far edge of the board. Begin sawing with a pull stroke to establish the location of the cut.

To use a radial-arm saw:

The board should be well supported along its length and held firmly against the fence. While the machine is still off, align the wood so that the blade will cut just to the waste side of the pencil line. Make sure the blade is not in contact with the wood and that your hands are clear of its path. Then turn the saw on and draw the blade by the handle across the wood. Offer enough resistance to keep the blade from pulling itself through. When the cut is complete, push the saw back to its starting position and turn the machine off.

The correct way to use a try square is to hold the stock firmly against the work.

When the end of the board is free of splits, measure out 25 in. in length and square a line across.

To measure:

This first measurement is only a rough one, where 1/16 in. or so won't matter. If you are using a tape measure, place the hook over the end of the board and pull the tape out from there. If you are using a folding rule, hold the end of the unfolded rule even with the end of the board. For measurements where greater accuracy is required, measure from the 1-in. mark on the tape or rule (see the photo at left). Make sure you measure to a number 1 in. greater than the one you actually want. Once in a while I forget to add the extra inch and come up with a piece of wood an inch too short.

Cut the board to length, again using a handsaw or radial-arm saw.

Measure from the 1-in. mark on a folding rule for measurements where greater accuracy is required. Remember to add the extra inch to your measurement.

STEP 2.   RIP TO APPROXIMATE WIDTH.

Next, rip the board to approximate width, using a hand rip saw, bandsaw or table saw. Leave at least 1/4 in. extra width over the 3 1/2 in. we are aiming for. I prefer to rip with a bandsaw, which is safer than a table saw and easier than a handsaw.

To rip with a bandsaw:

Rather than put a fence on the bandsaw, which requires setting the drift (see p. 44), I mark the width directly on the board with a pencil and straightedge, and bandsaw freehand.

Before you start ripping, make sure the blade of the bandsaw is square to the table. For safety, set the blade guard just above the thickness of the wood. Always push forward—if you pull the board back toward you in the middle of a bandsaw cut, you can pull the blade off the wheels.

To rip on the table saw:

Ripping rough lumber to width on a table saw is common practice, but more dangerous than using a bandsaw. A board that is warped or has curved edges (as rough lumber often does) has a greater chance of binding against the blade and kicking back. If you are ripping with a table saw, you should first look to see if the edge that will run against the rip fence is straight. If not, straighten it on a jointer before proceeding (see pp. 89-90).

a. Install a rip or combination blade and make sure it is set square to the table. If you have any doubt after checking the blade with a square, make a sample cut on a scrap board.

b. Set the rip fence to the desired width, about 3 3/4 in. away from the blade in this case. Measure the width as the distance from the fence to a saw tooth that hooks toward it (see the photo at top right on the facing page).

c. Raise the blade a tooth's height over the thickest part of the wood to be sawn.

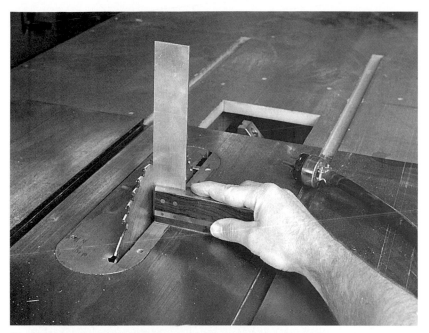

Use a square to check that the sawblade is square to the table.

Set the rip fence the desired distance from the sawblade.

Set the sawblade a tooth higher than the thickness of the wood.

d. If the board is cupped, put the convex side face down against the table. With the concave side down, the elevated center of the board would drop to the table at the completion of the cut, possibly binding between the blade and the fence. If the board is badly cupped, hold the section between the blade and the fence as flat as possible against the table.

e. Have a push stick handy to complete the cut.

f. Turn the saw on and feed the board through as steadily as possible. Keep the edge of the board against the fence at all times. To avoid binding and kickback, do not let go of the board under any circumstances until the cut is complete and the board has passed the sawblade.

g. Do not place your free hand on the wood beyond the blade, because it would be in a position to be drawn into the blade should a kickback occur.

h. Use the push stick to complete the cut, rather than passing your hand near the blade. The push stick should be centered on the section of wood that will pass between the blade and the fence. If the push stick is too close to the fence it can steer the front end of the board away from the fence, somewhat like the rudder of a boat.

To rip with a handsaw:

a. Mark the desired width on the board with a pencil and straightedge.

b. Be sure that you are using a rip saw. A crosscut saw is ineffectual for ripping.

c. Support the board across two sawhorses.

d. Saw up to, but not through, the line. Try to keep the sawn edge square to the face of the board.

Start the rip cut (top left) by pushing the wood forward through the blade with your right hand, while holding the board down on the saw table and firmly against the fence with your left hand. Continue holding the board in position with your left hand while reaching for a push stick with your right (middle left). Complete the cut by releasing your left hand and following through with the push stick until the board is completely beyond the sawblade (bottom left).

Gauge the depth of cut on a jointer by placing a straightedge flat on the outfeed table and extending it over the infeed table.

STEP 3. **FLATTEN ONE FACE.**

Once the board has been cut to approximate length and width, the next step is to flatten one face with a jointer or hand planes.

If you are using a jointer, be sure the knives are sharp and properly set. If not, refer to the machine's manual. The jointer's fence should be located at the far edge of the table, allowing access to virtually the full width of the knives. Only when the knives have been knicked or dulled at the far end, where they receive the most use, does the fence need to be moved to a narrower position.

To use a jointer:

a. Set the infeed table to take off no more than $\frac{1}{16}$ in. per pass. If necessary, you can gauge the depth of cut with a straightedge placed flat on the outfeed table and extending over the infeed table. Assuming the outfeed table is correctly set, tangent to the apex of the knives, the height of the straightedge off the infeed table equals the depth of cut. Usually, I gauge the depth of cut by the fcel of the first pass.

To flatten the first face on the jointer, hold the board down on the infeed table and against the fence with your left hand, while pushing it over the cutterhead with a push stick held in your right.

As the board passes over the cutterhead, transfer your weight to hold the board against the outfeed table. Follow through with the push stick in your right hand until the board is completely beyond the cutterhead.

b. Determine which face of the board you will joint. I prefer to flatten the more concave face because it sits more steadily on the table. But I also consider how the grain will run later, when I place the newly jointed face against the fence to square an edge in Step 4 (see pp. 93-95).

c. Decide in which direction the board should be fed in order to cut with the grain (see p. 8 and the drawing on p. 45).

d. Turn the machine on, place the board face down on the infeed table, and push the board through at a steady pace with its edge against the fence. Make sure you have a push stick handy. At the start of the cut, hold the board down on the infeed table. As the bulk of the board passes the cutterhead, shift your weight to the outfeed table. Don't alter the shape of a bowed board by forcing it flat against the jointer table—it will just spring back to its natural bow at the end of the pass.

e. Use a push stick to finish the cut, rather than passing your hand over the cutterhead.

f. Don't release the board before the cut is complete.

g. Take as many passes as necessary to remove all dips and hollows.

h. When the newly jointed face is completely smooth and flat, mark it with a pencil check mark for later reference.

The tools used to flatten the face of a board by hand are a flat workbench, a scrub plane and a long bench plane (for this project I used a 14-in. jack plane). The scrub plane is for quick wood removal during the initial stage of flattening wide or particularly warped boards. It can be dispensed with when planing a reasonably flat, small board such as the one we are working with in this exercise.

Hand planing may seem daunting at first, but it quickly becomes a pleasure. The secret is to have a well-tuned plane with a razor-sharp blade. Resharpen blades as soon as they start making dust rather than shavings (see pp. 78-81 for a discussion of grinding and sharpening). When planing, lift the plane off the wood on the return stroke to keep the blade sharp longer. When a plane is not in use, rest it on its side, rather than its sole, for the same reason.

Use winding sticks to check the board for twist.

To use hand planes:
a. Choose which side of the board to flatten. (I find it easier to flatten the more convex side first.)
b. Clamp the board flat on top of the workbench, preferably with bench dogs and a tail vise. If dogs aren't an option, hold the board in place by wedging it between thinner pieces of wood clamped across your workbench; avoid obstructing the path of your hand plane. If the board rocks, place small wedges underneath to hold it steady.
c. Examine the surface of the board with a straightedge to see where the high and low spots are. Use winding sticks (straight sticks of uniform width) to determine the degree of twist. Place a stick across each end of the board, parallel to each other. Sight across the tops of the sticks to reveal the amount of twist. (Skip to Step g if you are not using a scrub plane.)
d. Set the blade of your scrub plane to extend about 1/16 in. beyond the sole. To avoid tearout, plane across the grain or at a diagonal (see the top right photo on p. 132 for a scrub plane in use). Cover the entire surface of the board with parallel strokes. Try not to plane the lowest spots or you will diminish potential thickness.
e. Continue with the scrub plane, planing along the entire surface at the opposite diagonal. Keep switching directions until almost all of the surface has been affected. Most of the high spots will be gone.
f. Recheck flatness with the straightedge and winding sticks throughout the planing process. High spots can then be attacked with new vigor and low spots avoided.

Flatten the face of the board using a bench plane.

g. Switch to the bench plane. Begin planing at a diagonal or with the grain, whichever seems more appropriate. The valleys and ridges left by the curved blade of the scrub plane will disappear. Concentrate on the high areas. Finish up by planing along the length, with the grain. When the board is flat you will be able to take perfect, continuous shavings from one end to the other.

h. You are finished planing when the straightedge, winding sticks and shavings all tell you that the surface is flat. No trace of the original rough surface or the scrub planing should remain.

i. Mark the newly jointed face with a pencil for later reference.

Square the first edge to the previously flattened face on the jointer.

STEP 4. SQUARE ONE EDGE TO THE FLAT FACE.

Now that one face of the board is flat, that face becomes the reference against which one edge is straightened and squared with a jointer or hand plane.

To square an edge with a jointer:
a. Set the jointer fence square to the table. Check the angle of the fence with a square placed on the outfeed table just behind the cutterhead. Test the fence setting by jointing a piece of scrap.
b. Check the depth of cut. The jointer should remove no more than ¹⁄₁₆ in. at a pass. Thinner passes are less likely to cause tearout where the grain may change direction.
c. Turn the machine on and run the board through, cutting with the grain, if possible. Hold the flat face firmly against the fence and the board edge down on the table. Shift your weight from infeed to outfeed as the bulk of the board passes over the cutterhead.
d. If there is any danger of your fingers coming close to the cutterhead, use push sticks.
e. Take repeated passes until the edge of the board is uniformly milled.
f. Mark the newly jointed edge with a check mark for later reference.

SHOOTING BOARD FOR HAND PLANING

Clamp workpiece on narrower, top board, with edge to be planed overhanging.

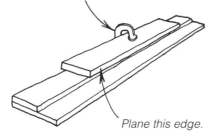

Plane this edge.

Squaring an edge freehand with a hand plane is difficult, so traditional woodworkers came up with a simple device to aid in this process. This is the shooting board (see the drawing at left), which consists of one flat, straight-edged board screwed onto a wider flat board. Sometimes, a stop is incorporated at one end of the top board.

To square an edge with a hand plane:

a. Clamp the work on the shooting board, flat face down. The edge to be planed should protrude a little beyond the edge of the narrower top board.

b. Set the iron of your longest bench plane to cut parallel with the sole. (A 24-in. jointer plane or one even longer works best.)

c. Begin planing the edge of the board. With the plane resting on its side, take long through strokes against the protruding edge. Hold the side of the plane firmly down on the shooting board to keep the angle constant.

d. When the entire edge has been planed, take a series of strokes that don't quite reach either end to make the edge slightly concave. Then take one or two full shavings all the way through. If you were preparing the board for edge-gluing, you could leave the edge slightly concave. What you wouldn't want is a convex edge, which would encourage the ends of the joint to spring open over time.

Sight down the jointer plane and set the blade parallel to the sole.

With the board clamped to the shooting board, plane along the entire length of the protruding edge.

e. Check the newly planed edge for squareness to the flat face. If it is off, adjust the angle of the plane iron accordingly and begin again.

f. When the edge is straight and square, mark it with a pencil for future reference.

STEP 5.   PLANE THE SECOND FACE PARALLEL TO THE FIRST.

At this point one face of the board is flat, one edge is flat and the two surfaces are square to each other. The second face and edge are still roughsawn and funky. If we were to flatten the second face on a jointer, as we did the first, we would have two flat sides that bore no particular relationship to each other. A jointer flattens a surface only in reference to itself; it doesn't know anything about the other side of the board.

We want to make the second face parallel to the first, in which case it will automatically be just as flat. This can be done with a thickness planer or with hand planes.

To use a thickness planer:

a. Check that the knives are sharp and properly set. If they are not, refer to the machine's manual.

b. Establish the correct depth of cut. With the machine turned off, adjust the opening between table and cutterhead so that it is wide enough for the board to pass through freely. Then raise the table or lower the cutterhead (whichever your machine does) until the thickest part of the board is slightly pinched under the infeed roller. Increase the opening just enough to remove the board, and re-close the gap.

c. Decide which end of the board should be fed in first to cut with the grain (see p. 8 and the drawing on p. 47).

d. Turn the machine on and feed the board in. Remember, the previously flattened side goes face down against the table; the rough side goes up to meet the cutterhead. The infeed roller will grab the board and pull it through. All you need to do is keep the board straight and catch it as it comes out the back.

e. Once you've made the first pass, reduce the distance between the cutterhead and the table by $\frac{1}{16}$ in. (or less) and take another pass. Depending on your planer, either a full turn or a half turn of the crank should be a $\frac{1}{16}$-in. adjustment.

f. Stop planing when the board measures the intended thickness.

Feed the board through the thickness planer to achieve the desired thickness.

Scribe the desired thickness around the edges of the board before hand-planing the second face.

To use hand planes:

a. Scribe the desired thickness around all four edges of the board with a marking gauge.

b. Clamp the board on the surface of the workbench between bench dogs, or wedge it in place.

c. Plane off most of the excess with a scrub plane. To avoid tearout, plane across the grain or at a diagonal.

d. Plane down to the scribed line with a long bench plane, working with the grain.

STEP 6. **RIP THE BOARD TO FINISHED WIDTH.**

One edge of the board remains to be cut to width, flattened and squared. I use a table saw for this step, but you could choose a handsaw or bandsaw and finish up with a bench plane.

To use a table saw, refer to Step 1 on pp. 86-88. Otherwise, mark the desired width on the board with a pencil and straightedge. If there is enough excess, cut carefully to (but not through) the line with a bandsaw or rip saw. After you saw (or if there was not enough excess to saw), plane to the line, straight and square, with the longest bench plane you have. Work freehand or with a shooting board. Remember to check the edge for squareness against the face as you go along.

Check the miter gauge for square before crosscutting the first end of the board.

Hold the board firmly against the miter-gauge fence and make the cut.

STEP 7. CUT ONE END SQUARE.

Our board now measures ¾ in. by 3½ in. and has four flat, straight sides that are square to one another. The next step is to cut one end square with a table saw, a chopsaw or a backsaw.

To use a table saw:

For crosscutting on a table saw, it is necessary to use a miter gauge or a sliding table. The rip fence should be well out of the way.

a. Set the blade square to the table and a tooth's height above the thickness of the wood.
b. If you are using a miter gauge, check it for square. A sliding table should always be square. If it is not square, either fix it or replace it. There is no use cluttering up the shop with inaccurate equipment.
c. Turn the machine on and make the cut. The board should be held firmly against the fence of the miter gauge or sliding table. You only need remove enough length to square the end. Make sure your fingers are not in the line of the cut. Remember, the blade will come through the back of the miter gauge or sliding table as you complete the cut.
d. Safely retrieve the workpiece. Once the cut has been made, you can either leave the board beyond the sawblade or pull it back to the starting position in one continuous motion. Don't stop with the wood in contact with the sawblade. Turn the machine off and let the blade stop spinning before you lift the board off the saw.
e. Check the end for square.

To use a chopsaw:

If you are using a chopsaw, hold the wood firmly against the fence and make sure that you keep your fingers out of the path of the blade. Check the result for squareness—not all chopsaws are well made or easily adjustable.

To use a backsaw:

There are two approaches to marking for a backsaw cut. For a less rigorous square end, like this one, it is fine to saw to a pencil line. For greater precision, as when sawing the shoulders of a joint, saw to a knife line.

a. Carefully square a line around one end of the board with a sharp pencil. Leave at least $3/16$ in. of waste on the outside of the line to help hold the saw in its kerf. Good work depends on good marking. The pencil lines should be fine and meet exactly at each corner.

b. Clamp the wood firmly in a vise or over the edge of a bench top.

c. Hold the saw at a diagonal on the near corner. Begin with a backstroke to establish the kerf. Saw down and across at the same time. Sawing on the face and edge simultaneously keeps the cut square in both dimensions. Saw to the line, not through it.

To cut the end of the board square with a backsaw, make the first saw cut on a diagonal.

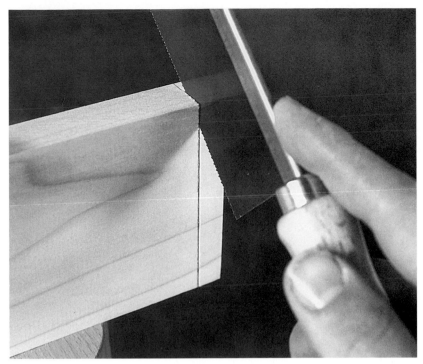

The second saw cut uses the kerf from the first saw cut as a guide down the face of the board.

d. Once the full diagonal is sawn, turn the board 90° toward you and make a new diagonal cut. The previous kerf will guide the saw down the face of the board.

e. When the second diagonal is complete, turn the board another 90° to saw the last face. Once again, saw a diagonal.

f. Place the saw straight across the kerf you just made and saw straight down till the end of the board falls off. The kerfs on either side will guide the saw if you let them.

Cutting a square end takes practice, so don't expect to get it right the first time. An imperfect job can be improved by paring the high spots with a chisel or a block plane.

STEP 8. **CUT THE OTHER END SQUARE AND TO LENGTH.**
The final step is to cut the second end square and to length. Measure out 24 in. from the square end. Use a square and pencil to mark the length around all four sides. Cut as you did in Step 7.

PROJECT 2:

CUTTING A MORTISE AND TENON

The mortise and tenon is the most important joint in fine furniture making. There is no stronger or more permanent means of joining two pieces of wood together in situations where the end of one board meets the edge of another. Mortise-and-tenon joints can be cut with hand tools, power tools or various combinations of the two.

Simple mortise-and-tenon joints that meet at right angles can be made satisfactorily with power tools, but the ability to cut a mortise and tenon by hand opens up a much wider range of applications and design possibilities. In this chapter we will go through the step-by-step process of cutting a simple, blind mortise and tenon by hand. The skills involved—measuring, marking, sawing, chopping and paring with chisels, sharpening and fitting—are basic building blocks of wood craftsmanship.

Don't expect your first, second or third mortise and tenon to be perfect. The first one may be terrible, but each subsequent one will be an improvement. Once you master the process, you will be technically and psychologically ready to learn any aspect of furniture making.

To prepare for this project, cut the piece of wood milled in the previous project in half to make two pieces ¾ in. by 3½ in. by approximately 12 in. long. The exact lengths aren't important, but make sure the ends come out square.

The experience of cutting a mortise and tenon is affected by the species of wood. A soft hardwood, such as poplar, cuts and assembles relatively easily; there is enough compressibility in the wood to forgive some fatness in the joint. A denser wood like cherry offers greater resistance to the saw and chisel, and must be cut to closer tolerances for a good fit, but it also works much cleaner and crisper.

CUTTING A MORTISE

Mortises are always cut before tenons, because there is more flexibility in sizing a tenon to fit a mortise than the other way around. The general rule for thickness is that a mortise should be approximately one-third as thick as the wood into which it is cut. The specific thickness of a hand-cut mortise is determined by the nearest size of chisel. For example, a mortise cut in a piece of ¾-in. wood should be ¼ in. thick, with ¼-in. shoulders on each side. A mortise cut in a piece of ⅞-in. wood could be either ¼ in. or ⁵⁄₁₆ in. thick, as long as you have both size chisels to choose from.

The depth of a mortise should be at least twice its thickness. The width can vary considerably. Our mortise will be ¼ in. thick, ⅝ in. deep and 2 in. wide, with ¾-in. shoulders at each end (see the drawing below).

MORTISE-AND-TENON PROPORTIONS

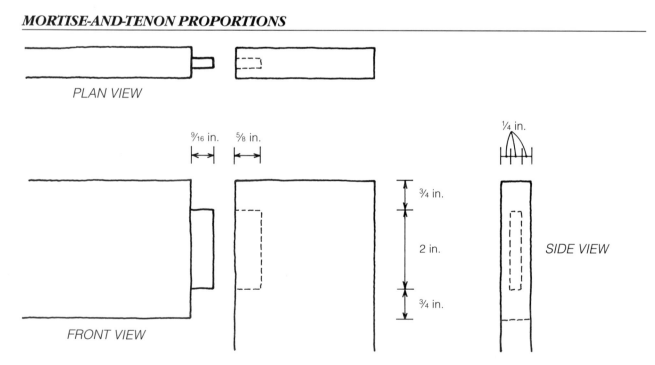

PLAN VIEW

⁹⁄₁₆ in. ⅝ in.

¼ in.

¾ in.

2 in.

¾ in.

SIDE VIEW

FRONT VIEW

There are many ways to cut a mortise. The most basic is to chop it out with mortising chisels and a mallet. At the other end of the spectrum, there are mortises machined with expensive equipment such as horizontal slot mortisers and hollow-chisel mortisers. Mortises can also be made with routers, as we shall see on pp. 186-187.

The tools required for cutting the mortise are a folding rule, mortising gauge, sharp knife, try or engineer's square, mallet, ¼-in. chisel, 1-in. or 1¼-in. chisel, drill press and ³⁄₁₆-in. brad-point drill bit.

The method presented here emphasizes hand skills, but employs a drill press for quick removal of waste. The steps are as follows:

1. MARK OUT THE MORTISE.

2. PARE BACK TO THE KNIFE LINE FROM WITHIN THE MORTISE.

3. DRILL OUT THE WASTE.

4. CHOP DOWN JUST SHY OF THE ENDS.

5. PARE DOWN THE SIDES AND REMOVE THE WASTE.

6. CHOP THE ENDS TO THE KNIFE LINE.

7. PARE THE SIDES SQUARE AND THE BOTTOM CLEAN.

Butt the tenon piece against the mortise piece and make a reference mark across the face of both boards.

Mark the mortise ends square across the edge of the board with a knife.

STEP 1. MARK OUT THE MORTISE.

First, decide which of the two pieces of ¾-in. by 3½-in. by 12-in. wood is for the mortise and which is for the tenon. Position them with the tenon piece butting against the mortise piece to form a corner. Mark the face of each board so you'll remember how they go together (see the photo above left). Later, when you use the mortising gauge, be sure to mark from the "face" side of each board. Scribing from the face of one and the back of the other would misalign the joint to the extent that the gauge wasn't perfectly centered.

To mark the mortise width, measure in ¾ in. and 2¾ in. from the end of the board, on the side where the mortise will be located. Mark each measurement with a knife prick. Square the marks across the wood with a knife.

To mark the mortise thickness, first set the mortising gauge. The distance between the pins (and from the shoulder of the gauge to the nearest pin) should be ¼ in. If the distance between the pins is less than ¼ in., the mortise will be too narrow to accommodate a ¼-in. chisel. With the shoulder of the gauge held firmly against the face of the board, scribe the thickness of the mortise from knife line to knife line, as shown in the top left photo on the facing page.

Scribe the mortise thickness with a mortising gauge.

Use a chisel to pare back to the knife lines at each end of the mortise.

For this project, there is no reason to have a perfectly centered mortise, but if you wanted one you would begin by setting the gauge as explained on the facing page. Then you would use it to make pin pricks from both faces of the board at one location. If the pricks coincided, the setting would be perfect. If not, you would readjust the fence of the gauge until they did coincide.

Save the setting on the mortising gauge for marking the tenon.

STEP 2.   PARE BACK TO THE KNIFE LINE.

Hold the wood between bench dogs, in a vise or clamped to the bench top. Working from the waste side, pare back to the knife lines at each end of the mortise with a sharp ¼-in. chisel. Pare with the bevel down for greater control. Paring creates a straight-backed groove that will guide the chisel while chopping the ends in Step 6 (see p. 108).

Whenever you pare with a chisel, keep both hands behind the blade. Time after time I have seen students ignore this advice and stab themselves. A bench dog, stop or vise should be used to hold the board, not a hand in front of the blade.

PARING BACK TO THE KNIFE LINE

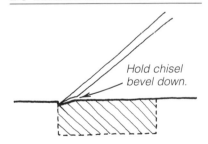

Hold chisel bevel down.

Paring back to the knife line creates a straight-backed groove that will guide the chisel in chopping the mortise ends.

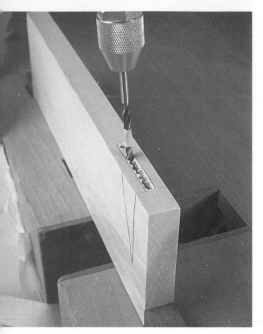

Drill out the mortise waste with a hand drill, electric drill or drill press. Masking tape wrapped around the drill bit indicates the desired depth of the mortise.

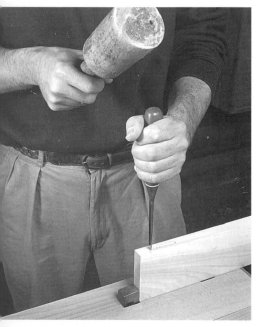

Chop down into the wood just shy of the mortise ends.

STEP 3.   DRILL OUT THE WASTE.

Drill out the waste with a brad-point bit smaller than ¼ in. in diameter. Begin with a hole near each end, then connect them with a series of contiguous holes. The holes should not impinge on the sides or ends of the mortise.

Use a drill press, electric drill or hand drill. If you are using a drill press, the edge of the board that sits on the table must be square to the sides; otherwise the holes will run crooked. The extension slide on a folding rule is useful for checking the depth of the first hole.

To use a drill press:
a. Make sure the table is set square to the bit. Adjust the height of the table to bring the wood close to the bit.
b. Set the depth stop to make holes that will go ⅝ in. beyond the surface of the wood.
c. When drilling a piece this size, hold the wood firmly on the drill table with your free hand. Smaller pieces, which might spin out of control, should be clamped in place or held against a fixed fence.
d. I usually eyeball the locations of the holes as I drill, but you may prefer to clamp a fence on the drill table as a guide. The holes don't have to be perfectly centered within the mortise.

To use an electric drill or hand drill:
a. Wrap masking tape around the drill bit, ⅝ in. from the cutting edge, to indicate the desired depth.
b. Clamp the wood firmly in a vise or to your bench.
c. Visually align the drill from the front and the side to make sure you are drilling as straight as possible.
d. If desired, scribe a line down the center of the mortise with a marking gauge to provide a pilot for the bit.

STEP 4.   CHOP DOWN JUST SHY OF THE ENDS.

Hold the wood on the bench top with bench dogs or a clamp. Chop down with a ¼-in. chisel (with the bevel facing inward) just in from each end of the mortise (see the photo at left). Drive the chisel with a mallet until it hits the bottom of the mortise. The little bit of meat left at each end will prevent the lip from being dented as waste is pried out of the mortise.

Although this mortise will be invisible once the joint is assembled, the goal is to have crisp, clean corners and edges. Good work is good work, whether or not it will be seen.

Pare down the sides of the mortise with a 1-in. or 1¼-in. bench chisel.

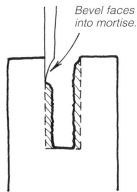

Bevel faces into mortise.

With a wide bench chisel, cut straight down the sides of the mortise.

STEP 5.   PARE DOWN THE SIDES.

Set a wide bench chisel, either 1 in. or 1¼ in., in either of the small grooves left by the mortising gauge. The bevel should face into the mortise. Gently tap the chisel with a mallet to cut straight down the side of the mortise. Don't drive the chisel too far, or the wood may split. The chisel should be razor sharp (for instructions on sharpening chisels, see pp. 78-81).

When you have cut partway down both sides in this fashion, use the ¼-in. chisel to clean out the waste as far down as the sides are pared. Resume paring the sides, cleaning out the waste as you go, until you reach the bottom of the mortise.

CUTTING A TENON

A tenon should fit a mortise snugly, like a hand in a glove. They should go together with noticeable friction, but not require serious pounding. An overly tight tenon can split a mortise along the grain.

The tools required for cutting a tenon with hand tools are a folding rule, mortising gauge, knife, square, backsaw, various chisels and a marking gauge or pencil.

There is more than one right way to cut a tenon. The method is largely a matter of personal preference. The following steps work well for me:

1. MEASURE AND MARK THE TENON LENGTH.

2. SCRIBE THE THICKNESS WITH A MORTISING GAUGE.

3. MARK THE WIDTH.

4. PARE BACK TO THE SHOULDERS.

5. SAW THE SHOULDERS WITH A BACKSAW.

6. SAW THE CHEEKS.

7. RE-MARK AND SAW THE WIDTH.

8. CLEAN UP AND FIT.

Mark the tenon shoulder across one face of the board with a knife.

Use the first cut to register the knife for the second cut on the side of the board.

STEP 1. MEASURE AND MARK THE TENON LENGTH.

The mortise is $\frac{5}{8}$ in. deep, so the tenon should be $\frac{9}{16}$ in. long to ensure that it doesn't hit bottom before the shoulders pull tight. With a sharp knife, mark the shoulder $\frac{9}{16}$ in. from the end of the tenon piece, and square the mark around all four sides.

Accuracy is extremely important when marking shoulders. Hold the stock of the square firmly against the wood, and hold the knife blade at a constant angle throughout each cut. The first cut is used to register the knife's position for the second cut, and so on. The last cut should meet the first cut perfectly.

For greatest accuracy in squaring a line around a board, always register the stock of the square against the jointed face and edge. If the other edge and face were not milled perfectly parallel to the jointed sides, the line will still come out right.

STEP 2. SCRIBE THE TENON THICKNESS.

The mortising gauge should still have the same setting that was used for the mortise. Clamp the wood upright in a vise so both your hands will be free. Place the fence of the gauge firmly against the face of the wood. Scribe the tenon thickness around the edges and end of the board, from shoulder to shoulder.

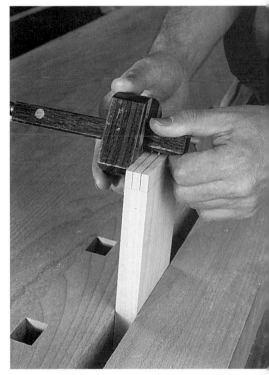

Scribe the tenon thickness from shoulder to shoulder with the mortising gauge.

STEP 3.   MARK THE WIDTH.

The width of a blind tenon does not need to be cut as perfectly as its thickness. The significant glue bond will be formed between the cheeks of the tenon and the sides of the mortise, where edge grain meets edge grain. The width serves primarily to register the tenon in place.

Tenon width can be marked with a marking gauge or a pencil and square. To use a marking gauge, clamp the wood upright in a vise. If you have accurately milled the wood to a width of 3½ in., set the gauge with the pin ¾ in. from the shoulder. Scribe the tenon width down both cheeks and across the end, working in from each side. The distance between the scribed lines should be 2 in.

To use a pencil and square, measure in ¾ in. from each side and square the width around.

STEP 4.   PARE BACK TO THE SHOULDERS.

Now that the tenon is completely marked out, the next step is to make a channel to guide the backsaw in cutting the shoulders.

Lay the wood flat on the workbench. Place a bench dog or stop at the far end to keep the wood from sliding away from you. On all four sides, pare a small groove back to the knifed shoulder line from the tenon side. Pare with the bevel down for greater control. Keep both hands behind the blade for safety.

STEP 5.   SAW THE SHOULDERS.

Hold the wood in a vise, or clamp it over the edge of your bench top. Start sawing on a diagonal at the corner nearest you. It is easier to begin with a couple of pull strokes. The saw teeth should rest against the knife line. Cut down and across at the same time. Working in two dimensions keeps the saw straight in both.

Saw all the way across the board and down to the nearest scribe mark, which denotes the location of the edge of the tenon. Don't saw the side of the board you can't see.

Rotate the board 90° toward you and saw on the diagonal once again. This time, there will be a kerf as a vertical guide. Stop sawing when you have cut all the way across on the horizontal and down to the nearest scribe line. Rotate the board and repeat the diagonal sawing process two more times. The kerfs on all four sides should go right up to the knifed shoulder, but not through it.

Finally, cut each shoulder down to the level of the tenon, with the saw held horizontally. The existing kerfs will guide the saw.

Scribe the tenon width using a marking gauge from each side.

Pare back to the knife line on all four sides of the board.

Starting at the near corner, saw the tenon shoulders on the diagonal.

Saw the tenon cheeks on the diagonal.

STEP 6.   SAW THE CHEEKS.

Place the wood in a vise on an upright diagonal leaning away from you. Saw on the waste sides of the tenon, up to, but not through, the scribe marks left by the mortising gauge. Saw down and across simultaneously for greater control. Stop when you have cut across the end and down to the shoulder. Don't saw on the side you can't see.

Turn the board around and place it upright in the vise. Cut down the second side with the saw straight across. The existing kerfs will guide the saw, if you let them. When you reach the shoulder, the waste pieces should fall off the cheeks. If not, the shoulder wasn't sawn deep enough in the previous step.

STEP 7.   RE-MARK AND SAW THE WIDTH.

When the cheek waste falls off, the width marks go with it. Re-mark the width with the marking gauge or a pencil and square. Then saw to the lines. Begin sawing on a diagonal, but finish straight across. This entire cut can be done from one side.

STEP 8.   CLEAN UP AND FIT.

Once a tenon is sawn, a certain amount of cleanup is usually necessary. First, check for high spots on the shoulders with a straightedge—the edge of a chisel works fine. Pare off any high spots so the straightedge rests on the shoulders without rocking. Slight back-cutting (paring the interior lower than the edges) is permissible.

The completed mortise and tenon.

An alternative way to flatten the shoulders is to use a rabbet plane, referencing the body of the planc against the cheeks of the tenon to keep the shoulders square.

Next, try to fit the tenon into the mortise. If it is too thick or too wide, pare it down methodically to maintain squareness. Again, remember to clamp the wood or hold it in a vise while paring. Keep the back of the chisel flat against the wood to tell you where the high spots are. Pare with or across the grain, where possible, rather than against it.

The assembled joint should have a firm fit with snug shoulders. If the shoulders are not snug, either the tenon is too long or the shoulders are not flat. If the shoulders are snug on one side only, the off shoulder may not be quite flat, or the mortise or the tenon may be angled and require further paring.

If you feel there is room for improvement, begin again. Cut off the tenon to make the end square. Mark a mortise in a new location. Sharpen your chisels. Work carefully. Each step builds on the accuracy of the previous ones.

With a reasonable commitment to practice you will master the skill of cutting a mortise and tenon with hand tools. Once you can do that, you can do anything!

PROJECT 3:

CUTTING DOVETAILS

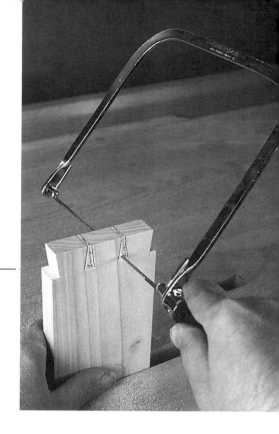

Cutting dovetails by hand involves the same skills as cutting a mortise and tenon. However, dovetails are more complex to visualize and more exacting to cut. This chapter presents the step-by-step process for cutting through dovetails, as a means of consolidating and building upon the skills learned in the previous project.

Whereas mortise-and-tenon joinery is used primarily for frames, seating and other situations in which the end of one piece of wood butts into the side of another, dovetails are used for carcase construction (boxes, drawers, dressers, etc.), where two pieces of wood meet end to end to form a corner. Taken together, the mortise and tenon and the dovetail form the cornerstone of traditional wood joinery and are unsurpassed in effectiveness and quality.

Dovetails can be cut with a template and router as quickly and accurately as they can by hand. But the predetermined proportion and regularity of machined dovetails aesthetically diminishes the work, compared to the harmonies of spacing and proportion that are possible with hand-cut dovetails.

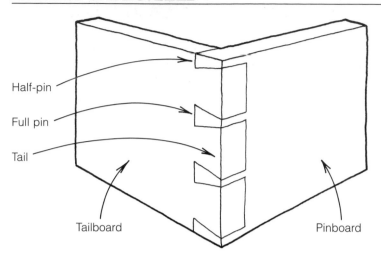

Half-pin

Full pin

Tail

Tailboard

Pinboard

HOW A ONE-IN-SEVEN ANGLE IS LAID OUT

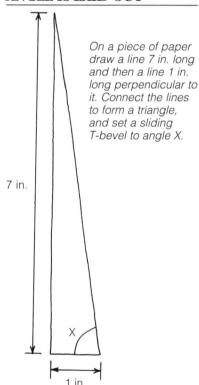

On a piece of paper draw a line 7 in. long and then a line 1 in. long perpendicular to it. Connect the lines to form a triangle, and set a sliding T-bevel to angle X.

7 in.

X

1 in.

There are infinite combinations of tail and pin thicknesses, spacings and angles at which dovetails can be cut (see the drawing on p. 120). The choice depends on the maker's aesthetic preference, but tradition provides some guidelines:

- A dovetail joint always begins and ends with pins (see the drawing above). The pins at either end are called "half-pins" because only their interior sides are angled.
- Tail and pin size may vary within a joint, but the tails and pins are usually spaced symmetrically.
- In a wide joint, the outer tails are often smaller than the ones in the middle of the board. Small tails provide greater holding power against cupping.
- The narrowness of pins has traditionally been a way for furniture makers to show off their skill. A good craftsman can cut pins that taper to less than $\frac{1}{16}$ in. at the base.
- The angles at which dovetails are cut are traditionally described as one-in-six, one-in-seven or one-in-eight. The steeper degree of physical interlock provided by one-in-six dovetails offers greater mechanical resistance to being pulled apart. The slighter slope of one-in-eight dovetails is thought of as more decorative and pleasing to the eye. I usually cut one-in-seven dovetails, which I find a good compromise between strength and beauty.

CUTTING THROUGH DOVETAILS

There are many methods for cutting dovetails by hand. Woodworkers are an idiosyncratic lot, but we all divide into two basic camps—those who cut tails first and those who begin with pins. My preference is to start with the tails, but I encourage you to experiment with both approaches and make up your own mind.

To prepare for this project, mill another piece of hardwood measuring ¾ in. by 3½ in. by 24 in. and cut it in half to make two pieces with square ends, each about 12 in. long. (Refer back to Project 1 on pp. 83-99.) It will be easier to see layout marks on a light-colored wood.

The steps we will use to cut through dovetails are:

1. MARK THE SHOULDERS FOR THE TAILS AND PINS.

2. LAY OUT THE TAILS.

3. PARE BACK TO THE TAIL SHOULDERS.

4. SAW THE TAILS.

5. CHOP THE SHOULDERS OF THE TAILS.

6. LAY OUT THE PINS, USING THE TAILS AS A TEMPLATE.

7. PARE BACK TO THE PIN SHOULDERS.

8. CUT THE PINS AND CHOP THE SHOULDERS.

9. FIT THE JOINT TOGETHER.

10. PLANE THE ENDS FLUSH.

Mark the shoulders for the tails and pins with a shallow knife line.

The tools required include a folding rule, knife, square, sliding T-bevel, various chisels, backsaw, coping saw, a very sharp pencil and a block plane or file. An awl is optional.

STEP 1. MARK THE SHOULDERS FOR TAILS AND PINS.

First, choose which ends of the two boards will meet to form the joint, and designate one board for tails and the other for pins. Mark the boards with a pencil so you'll remember how they go together. Make sure the ends are square.

Through dovetails can be flush or proud. But even when making flush dovetails, as we will here, the tails and pins are generally cut a hair proud to start with and planed flat after assembly. That way, small imperfections left on the board ends from marking, sawing or chiseling can be eliminated.

To mark the shoulders for the tails and pins, measure in from each board end about $1/16$ in. more than the thickness of the mating piece—$13/16$ in. in this case. Lightly square the mark around all four shoulders with a knife. The knife line should be shallow, since it will be visible on the outside of the completed joint where it crosses the tails and pins. Some furniture makers leave the knife line, especially on drawer sides. Others plane out the lines once the joint is assembled.

STEP 2. LAY OUT THE TAILS.

You may want to draw a series of possible dovetail variations with pencil and paper before deciding on the final angle and spacings. The base of each tail, and the spaces between them, should be at least as wide as your narrowest chisel (which is probably $1/4$ in.); otherwise, it will be difficult to clean out the shoulders.

DOVETAIL VARIATIONS

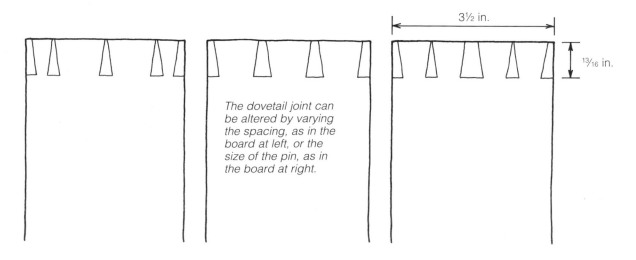

3½ in.

$13/16$ in.

The dovetail joint can be altered by varying the spacing, as in the board at left, or the size of the pin, as in the board at right.

Once you have decided on a pattern, set the angle of a sliding T-bevel to the pitch you have chosen. With a very sharp pencil, mark the tails on one face of the designated tailboard. The thinner the pencil lines, the easier it will be to saw precisely.

Transfer the lines across the end of the board with a square and pencil, then mark them down the other side with the T-bevel. Be careful to align the lines at the edges and to keep the pencil sharp.

Finally, mark the waste areas between the tails with a pencil to avoid mistakes such as sawing to the wrong side of a line. From time to time, I encounter a student who has removed the tails and left the waste areas. What's worse, he usually doesn't discover the mistake until he has cut reverse pins on the other piece and wonders why the two boards don't interlock the way they should.

STEP 3.   PARE BACK TO THE TAIL SHOULDERS.

Pare a small groove back to the shoulders, from the tail side of the line, in the waste areas between the tails and around the outside edges. The groove will guide the chisel when chopping the shoulders in Step 5 (see p. 122).

STEP 4.   SAW THE TAILS.

To saw the tails, hold the wood upright in a vise. Sawing is easier if the wood is angled so that the lines marking one side of each tail are vertical. Saw the vertical set of lines with a backsaw. Cut from the waste side to, but not through, the pencil mark. Saw down and across simultaneously until you have completed a diagonal cut.

Use a sliding T-bevel and pencil to lay out the tails.

Pare back to the shoulders in the waste areas.

Saw the tails with the board held in a vise.

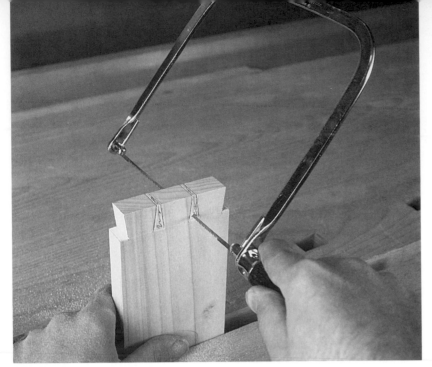

Use a coping saw to remove waste from between the tails.

With a sharp chisel, chop the tail shoulders square.

Change the angle of the board to make the other set of tail marks vertical and saw them on the diagonal as well. Turn the board around in the vise and, with the saw horizontal, saw each set of tail marks down to the shoulder. Next, use a coping saw to remove as much of the waste as possible from between the tails. Avoid cutting into the tails or shoulders.

STEP 5. CHOP THE SHOULDERS OF THE TAILS.

Hold the board flat on the bench with dogs or clamps and chop the shoulders square with a sharp chisel and mallet. Use the groove that you pared in Step 3 to position the chisel.

If there is more than $\frac{1}{16}$ in. to remove, make the first chop slightly shy of the shoulder; otherwise, the resistance of the waste wood can cause the chisel to dent the shoulder. For the same reason, use as wide a chisel as possible to spread resistance over more of the shoulder.

Chop halfway down. Then turn the board over and chop from the other side. You can expect some tearout as you come down the second side, but it should be invisible in the assembled joint. The angled corners where the tails intersect the shoulders should be cleaned out precisely.

Use the chisel as a straightedge to make sure the shoulders are flat across. The chisel should rest on the outside edges, not rock on a hump in the middle. Slight back-cutting is permissible between the edges.

Use the tailboard as a template to lay out the pins.

STEP 6. LAY OUT THE PINS.

Now that the tails are cleanly cut, you can use them as a template to mark the pins. Place the tailboard flat across a couple of pieces of wood on the bench top. Clamp the pinboard upright in a bench vise so it butts up against the underside of the tailboard. Put the shoulder of the tailboard in exact alignment with the inner edge of the pinboard. You may want to clamp the tailboard in place so it won't move while you are marking.

Trace the tails onto the pinboard piece with a sharp pencil, awl or knife. It can be difficult to mark accurately against the tails when they are close together. I use a lead holder with the lead well extended.

Once you have traced the tails, remove the tailboard. If your tracings are hard to read, use a straightedge to firm up the marks. Next, carefully square the marks down both faces, to the shoulders, with a sharp pencil or an awl. Now that the pins are laid out, indicate the waste areas in between with pencil marks.

STEP 7. PARE BACK TO THE PIN SHOULDERS.

Pare a small groove back to the shoulders in the waste areas between the pins, just as we did on the tailboard in Step 3 (see the photo at bottom left on p. 121).

Cut the pins with a backsaw.

The assembled dovetail joint, before being trimmed flush.

STEP 8.   CUT THE PINS AND CHOP THE SHOULDERS.

Hold the pinboard upright in a vise and cut the pins with a backsaw (see the photo above left). Saw them all on the diagonal from the first side, then turn the board around and saw horizontally down to the shoulder. Saw on the waste side up to, but not through, the lines, which are on the part of the pins that should snug up against the tails. Remove the waste with a coping saw.

Chop the shoulders, cutting in halfway from each side as in Step 5 (p. 122). Make sure the shoulders are straight across and the corners are cleaned out thoroughly.

STEP 9.   FIT THE JOINT TOGETHER.

Rarely does a dovetail joint fit together perfectly at this point. A certain amount of paring is inevitably required.

Hold the pins upright in a vise while you attempt to fit the joint together. Observe the tight spots and pare them gradually. If the tails were cut square across to start with, leave them alone and do all your paring on the pins.

The joint should go together without the assistance of a hammer; light taps from a rubber mallet should provide adequate encouragement. A well-cut dovetail has no visible gaps whatsoever.

If the joint does not fit perfectly, there are probably logical reasons. Rarely does an evil shop demon actually cast a spell on your saw. Problems can be traced to inaccurate marking, inaccurate sawing or shoulders and edges that have not been pared straight across.

Plane the tails flush with a block plane, working away from the corner of the joint to avoid splintering the wood.

STEP 10. PLANE THE ENDS FLUSH.

The last step is to make the pins and tails flush. Normally, this is done after the joint has been glued together. For the sake of practice, though, we can dispense with the glue. That way, the joint can be pulled apart and the ends cut off for a fresh start.

Hold the assembled joint in a vise and make the joint flush with a sharp block plane and/or a file. Whichever you are using, work away from the outside corner of the joint to avoid splintering the wood at the edge.

Don't despair if your first set of dovetails looks something like a smile with most of the teeth missing. Mine certainly did. I gave my first dovetailed box to my grandmother, who took every opportunity to show it off to her friends. A year's practice later, I was so embarrassed by those dovetails that I borrowed the box back and burned it in the fireplace. Unfortunately, my grandmother died before I could make her a new one.

Practice and patience are necessary to master the skill of cutting dovetails. Don't hesitate to cut fresh ends and start again. Mark carefully, use a sharp pencil, and saw to the lines; by the fourth or fifth attempt, the results will please you.

BUILDING
A SMALL
BENCH

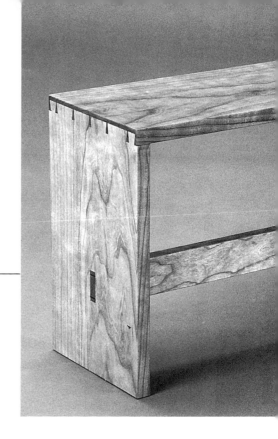

The bench presented in this chapter builds upon the skills learned
in previous projects and takes you through the entire furniture-
making process, from design to finishing. The bench is joined with
half-blind dovetails and through-wedged mortise and tenons.

Feel free to play with the proportions of the bench (the dimensions
I used are shown in the drawing on p. 129). Maybe you want a wider
or longer bench. Is it high enough? Is the stretcher in the right place?
Although I hope that you build this first bench with only minor
variations, I also encourage you to begin designing your own projects
as soon as possible.

THE DESIGN PROCESS

Designing your own furniture is one of the most rewarding aspects of
craftsmanship, but even skilled woodworkers sometimes treat
furniture design as a mystery on the order of nuclear physics: "Oh,
gosh, not me. I can't draw."

SMALL BENCH

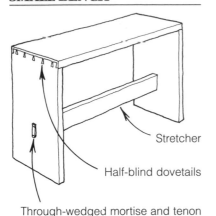

Stretcher

Half-blind dovetails

Through-wedged mortise and tenon

The first thing to do is sit down and start doodling on a scrap of paper. Doodling is the secret of design inspiration! Extensive doodling often leads to a state known as "letting the pencil do the thinking"—a designer's euphemism for total mindlessness—where ideas seem to appear on paper of their own accord.

Let's say you want to design a small bench to go by your fireplace. Set aside a half-hour or more of undisturbed time, and simply start sketching bench ideas with pencil and paper. Don't worry about drawing ability. You are the only person who has to understand your sketches. Don't stop to evaluate. Keep sketching. After a while you should begin to see some interesting ideas. I sometimes need several sketching sessions to come up with an idea that I want to pursue.

When you have created one sketch that is particularly appealing, the hard part is done. The rest of the design process consists of translating the sketch into reality by refining the concept and working out the details without sacrificing its charm.

First, decide on the bench's measurements. Examine existing benches as references for scale and proportion. After a while, design and construction details that ensure function, strength and durability can be induced from experience. In the meantime, the best way to learn is through observation.

Make scale drawings of your design. Use a parallel-bar drawing board, a T-square or even graph paper. An architect's rule makes it easy to work at scales from one-eighth to one-half of life size. A scale of ⅛ in. to 1 in. is appropriate for most furniture, but a small piece like the bench in this project could also be drawn on a larger scale, such as ¼ in. to 1 in.

Scale drawings show front and side views, as well as a plan (top) view. All three views are presented flat, without any attempt at creating a sense of perspective. Dotted lines indicate features hidden behind immediate surfaces. If a piece of furniture is symmetrical, you need only draw half the piece, indicating the axis of symmetry with a line labeled "CL" for centerline.

Once you are satisfied with the scale drawing, make a full-scale one that contains all the information required to build the piece. Full-scale drawings are laid out just like scale drawings, with front and side views and a plan view. Draw out every joinery detail to avoid mistakes later. Two advantages of full-scale drawings are that measurements can be taken directly from them and that they can be used to trace templates for curved pieces. They also preserve the information, should you ever decide to build the piece again. The only furniture for which I don't make full-scale drawings are pieces that are either too large to fit my drawing board or too simple to require anything more than a scale representation. My full-scale drawing board is a sheet of plywood used along with a 42-in. T-square.

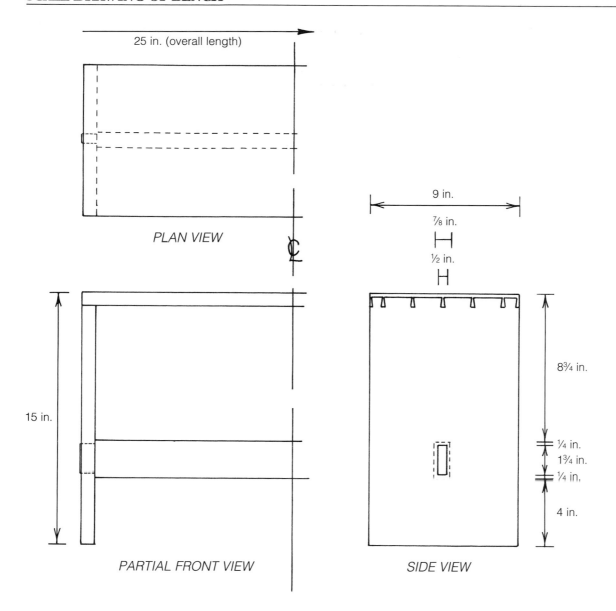

25 in. (overall length)

PLAN VIEW

9 in.

⅞ in.

½ in.

15 in.

PARTIAL FRONT VIEW

8¾ in.

¼ in.
1¾ in.
¼ in.
4 in.

SIDE VIEW

For presentation to a customer, I often draw perspective renderings, but I rarely do them just for myself. An accurate perspective rendering takes a lot of time, but only gives information from a single vantage point. Mock-ups are more informative. If a piece of furniture, particularly a chair, is too complex to be visualized from flat views, build a mock-up before putting extensive time into a finished product.

- 1 piece at $\frac{7}{8}$ in. x 9 in. x 25$\frac{1}{8}$ in. (bench top, including $\frac{1}{16}$-in. waste at each end)
- 2 pieces at $\frac{7}{8}$ in. x 9 in. x 14$\frac{3}{4}$ in. (legs, exact length).
- 1 piece at $\frac{7}{8}$ in. x 2$\frac{1}{4}$ in. x 25$\frac{1}{8}$ in. (stretcher, including through tenons with $\frac{1}{16}$ in. to spare at either end)

MAKING A CUTTING LIST

When a design has been worked out through full-scale drawings, the next step is to make a cutting list to indicate the size to which each component should be milled. Widths and thicknesses are usually given at their intended finished dimensions. Lengths should include tenons and allowances for waste that will be removed after the joinery is assembled.

Not all components have to be cut to exact length at this point. You might leave the bench legs an inch or so long to allow for mistakes; if your first set of dovetails doesn't come out well, you could cut them off and begin again. Leave the stretcher a little long, too. The stretcher's true length will depend upon the exact distance between the shoulders of the pins cut in the bench top, not the theoretical distance indicated by a drawing.

SELECTING THE LUMBER

Criteria for choosing the species of wood for a project can include color, grain, strength, cost and availability. Some furniture makers like to mix different woods together; others prefer to use a single species per piece. Some like the contrast provided by sapwood; others, like myself, use only heartwood.

My own preference has been to work from a palette of domestic hardwoods: cherry, ash, maple and walnut. Among these four woods I can almost always find a color and grain pattern to complement the design I am working on. The lighter woods, ash and maple, are more casual. Walnut has an air of seriousness. The pronounced grain of ash emphasizes the woodiness of a piece, while the finer grains of maple or cherry compete less with the form. All four woods are strong, but ash is more supple where bending is involved.

My favorite wood is cherry. There is an informal elegance to cherry that harmonizes with my idea of domesticity. Neither too light nor too dark, the fine grain lets you know it is wood without shouting about it. Cherry works cleanly and crisply, with relatively little tendency to tear out, and the small pores take a finish well. Also, cherry is readily available, and harvesting cherry does not destroy irreplaceable wildlife habitats.

Once you have chosen a species for your bench, select the board or boards you will use. When possible, I take an entire piece of furniture out of one board, or boards from the same tree, so the color and grain will match throughout.

All four parts of the bench are drawn to be ⅞ in. thick. To be sure of ending up at this dimension, I would start with a piece of 5/4 lumber. But, sometimes, I might take a piece of straight, roughsawn 4/4 lumber and get as much thickness out of it as possible, perhaps ending up with ¹³⁄₁₆ in. after the dust has settled. (I rarely use ¾-in. thick wood for furniture. As the standard thickness of construction materials, it is so familiar to the eye that it gives a commonplace look to a handmade object.)

Whatever wood you choose, look it over for surface cracks, end checks, sapwood, knots, bow, cup and twist (see pp. 9-11). No craftsman ever finds a perfect board; we just do the best with what we have.

Before cutting the wood, you have a number of decisions to make:
- Can the full width of the bench come out of one board?
- Can the bench be cut out of a single board so that the grain pattern continues up one leg, along the top and down the other leg?
- Is the rough lumber straight enough to mill the top and legs as a single board without having it get too thin? Or should the top and legs be cut apart and milled separately to conserve thickness?
- Which section of the board has the symmetry, pattern and color to make the best bench top?
- Are sapwood or knots acceptable?
- Will the first face be flattened with a jointer or a hand plane? Even if the board is too wide for the capacity of your jointer, it can be ripped in half, joined, thicknessed and glued back together again, as explained on pp. 133-134.

MILLING THE LUMBER

Once you have answered the questions above, mark the rough lumber, cut it in sections and mill it four-square to finish thickness and width, as explained in Project 1 (pp. 83-99).

Milling the stretcher involves the same straightforward process we encountered in Project 1. The bench top and legs can be more challenging, especially if you are trying to get them out of one piece of wood so that the grain matches all the way around.

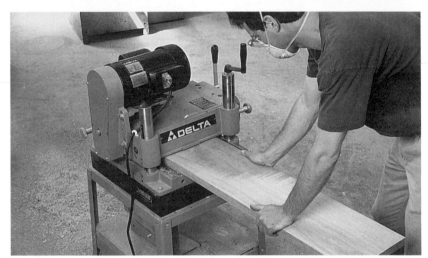

Plane the first face flat, starting with a scrub plane, if necessary (as shown).

Thickness-plane the second face of the board.

Cut the roughsawn board to approximate length on the radial-arm saw (top), then bandsaw the board to approximate width (above).

Joint one edge of the board square to the first face.

*Crosscut the board to finished length
using a sliding table on the table saw.*

Rip the board to finished width on a table saw.

The photos on pp. 132-133 show one method of milling the legs and top to size. The first face is hand-planed flat, the second face is machined flat in the thickness planer, one edge is squared on the jointer, and the board is cut to width on a table saw. The legs and top are milled to thickness and width as one board, then cut into separate parts. Had they been cut into separate parts before milling, the process would still have been the same.

An alternative method of milling the top and legs would be to cut the rough lumber in half lengthwise, so the first face could be flattened with a 6-in. or 8-in. jointer instead of a hand plane. Using this method, the steps would be:

1. Cut the rough wood to approximate length.
2. Saw the board in half lengthwise with a bandsaw, table saw or hand rip saw.
3. Flatten the first face of each half on the jointer.
4. Thickness-plane both boards to finished thickness (⅞ in. in this case).
5. Use the jointer to square the inside edge of each board—the edges that will meet at the center when the board is reassembled. (You can compensate for an imperfectly square jointer fence by running the face of one board and the back of the other against it. When the boards are reassembled, any angle left on the edges by the jointer will cancel itself out.)
6. Cut both boards to a width of 4½ in. on the table saw, so that their combined width is 9 in.
7. Glue the two boards back together, making sure their surfaces line up flush, and let the glue dry overnight.
8. Cut the reassembled board to length on the table saw.

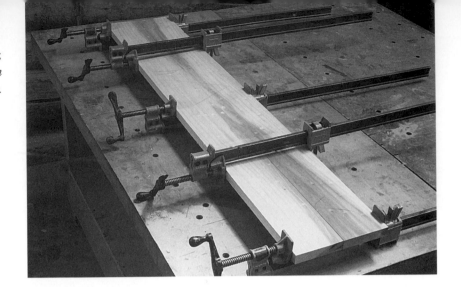

Edge-gluing two boards together, with clamps alternating on both sides.

If you choose to follow this alternative method of milling, you should read the section on gluing and assembly (pp. 152-156), as well as the following notes:

- To line up edges while gluing, some woodworkers insert dowels, splines or biscuits. I usually take the riskier (and faster) road of aligning the edges by hand as I clamp the boards together. Occasionally, glue sets before the boards are in position, but most of the time everything works out fine.
- Boards tend to arch under the pressure of clamping when their edges aren't square, the wood is thin or the clamps have too much flex. If possible, glue wide panels together with bar clamps, which have the least flex under pressure. Placing adjacent clamps on alternate sides of the panel offsets the tendency of the boards to arch (see the photo above). Another trick is to hold glued and clamped boards flat between pairs of straight sticks clamped across them.
- Newly glued boards should be left alone for a day or two before smoothing the joint. If moisture introduced by glue hasn't had time to evaporate, a planed joint continues to shrink, creating a depression.

At the conclusion of the milling process you will have four four-square pieces of wood cut to the sizes indicated on the cutting list. The legs and stretcher should be a little long, and the top should be exact. The ends of the top and legs should be perfectly square to facilitate cutting the dovetails.

After a piece of wood has been milled flat, take care to keep its faces from uneven exposure to moisture or heat. Otherwise, the board will cup. When I am not working on milled components, I stand them on edge, so that both faces are exposed to the air. Don't leave wood in the path of a hot-air heater or direct sunlight.

CUTTING HALF-BLIND DOVETAILS

Depending on your aesthetic preference, you can join the legs to the bench top with either through or half-blind dovetails. I designed this bench with half-blind dovetails because I like the way they leave the top surface uninterrupted.

The tools you will need for this project include a marking gauge, folding rule, knife, sharp pencil, backsaw, square, various chisels, mallet and sliding T-bevel. You will also need a drill and brad-point drill bits in various sizes.

The steps for cutting half-blind dovetails are as follows:

1. ORIENT THE LEGS AND THE TOP TO ONE ANOTHER.

2. MARK THE TAIL SHOULDERS.

3. LAY OUT THE TAILS.

4. PARE BACK TO THE TAIL SHOULDERS IN THE WASTE AREAS.

5. SAW THE TAILS AND CHOP THE SHOULDERS.

6. MARK THE PIN SHOULDERS.

7. MARK THE PIN DEPTH.

8. LAY OUT THE PINS FROM THE TAILS.

9. PARE BACK TO THE PIN SHOULDERS.

10. SAW THE PINS.

11. DRILL OUT THE WASTE.

12. CHOP THE PIN SHOULDERS AND PARE OUT THE WASTE.

13. FIT THE JOINT.

*Mark the tail shoulders on the legs
with a marking gauge set to ⅝ in.*

Use a sliding T-bevel to lay out the tails.

STEP 1. ORIENT THE LEGS AND THE TOP.

Place the parts of the bench in their relative positions and mark them with a pencil so there will be no confusion as to how they go together.

STEP 2. MARK THE TAIL SHOULDERS.

Set a marking gauge to scribe the length of the dovetails on the legs. The gauge's pin should be filed to cut like a knife. The length of the tails must allow for the thickness of wood that will remain between them and the top surface of the bench. If the bench stock is ⅞ in. thick and you plan to leave ¼ in. on the pin piece, the gauge should be set to mark ⅝-in. tails.

Marking and cutting the dovetails for both ends of the bench at the same time increases efficiency. Lightly mark the shoulders around all four sides of both legs, holding the fence of the gauge against the ends of the boards. This light scribe line will be deepened later in the waste areas. Where it crosses the base of the tails, the line will be planed off after assembly.

Save the setting on the gauge to mark out the pins.

Transfer the layout of the tails from one leg to the other.

Pare back to the shoulders between the tails.

STEP 3.   LAY OUT THE TAILS.

Lay out the tails in whatever pattern you like. Refer to the guidelines on pp. 120-121. When the tails on one leg have been marked around both sides and the end, transfer them to the other leg by squaring the end marks across. Be sure to identify waste areas clearly with pencil marks.

STEP 4.   PARE BACK TO THE TAIL SHOULDERS.

Use the marking gauge to cut the shoulder lines more deeply in the areas where waste will be removed. Pare back to the shoulders from the waste areas to form straight-backed grooves.

Use a backsaw to saw the tails.

Mark the shoulders for the pins on the bottom side of the bench.

STEP 5.   SAW THE TAILS AND CHOP THE SHOULDERS.
Saw the tails with a backsaw and chop out the waste areas, as explained on pp. 121-122.

STEP 6.   MARK THE PIN SHOULDERS.
Mark the shoulders for the pins with a knife and square. Pin shoulders are marked only on the bottom side of the bench. Each pin shoulder should be set in from the end of the board at least a hair deeper than the thickness of a leg. The overall length of the bench will be the distance between the pin shoulders at each end, plus the combined thickness of the legs.

STEP 7.   MARK THE PIN DEPTH.
With the marking gauge at the same setting used to scribe the length of the dovetails, mark the depth of the pins. Place the fence of the gauge against the underside of the bench top and scribe a line across each end.

Scribe pin depth with the marking gauge.

Use the tailboard as a template to lay out the pins.

STEP 8. LAY OUT THE PINS FROM THE TAILS.

Use the tails as a template to mark the pins, as described on p. 123. Since these are half-blind dovetails, the pins are squared down the bottom face of the board only. Mark the waste areas between the pins with a pencil.

STEP 9. PARE BACK TO THE PIN SHOULDERS.

Pare back to the shoulders in the waste areas between the pins.

STEP 10. SAW THE PINS.

Using a backsaw, cut the pins on the diagonal, from the shoulder to the depth mark. Saw on the waste side of the pins; saw to, but not through, their outlines.

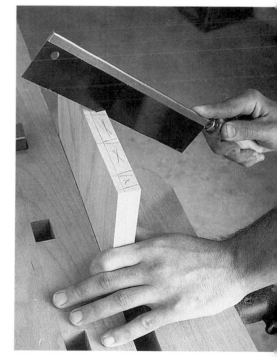

Saw the pins on the diagonal.

Drill out the bulk of the waste between the pins.

Working with the chisel parallel to the workbench, pare out the waste between the pins.

STEP 11. **DRILL OUT THE WASTE.**

Use a drill press or hand drill to remove most of the waste between the pins. If you are using a drill press, set the depth stop to a hair less than the finished depth of the pins. If you are using a hand drill, wrap masking tape around the bit as a depth indicator.

STEP 12. **CHOP THE SHOULDERS AND PARE THE WASTE.**

At this point, clamp the pinboard on the bench top about 2 in. from the edge. This way, you can keep the pin bottoms flat by paring out the waste with the chisel parallel to the bench.

Begin by chopping a false shoulder about ¹⁄₁₆ in. in from the real one, so that you can pry out waste without denting the real shoulder. Next, split out the waste, from the end, with a chisel and mallet. Don't try to get it all out in one chunk; work your way down about ⅛ in. at a time. Before you reach the bottom, clean out all interior corners. When the corners are clear, chop the final shoulder and pare the true bottom.

Paring the waste at the bottom can be difficult when the grain runs the wrong way. To minimize tearout when working against the grain, take thin cuts and pare with a side-to-side motion rather than straight in, if possible.

The completed pins should have crisp interior corners and flat sides. Shoulders and bottoms can be back-cut slightly for an easier fit, if necessary.

STEP 13. FIT THE JOINTS.

Try to assemble the dovetails. Light taps with a rubber mallet should provide sufficient force. Too tight a fit will cause the wood to split, so take your time in assessing tight spots. If the tails are already cleanly cut and square across, paring should take place on the pins.

When both dovetail joints fit to your satisfaction, disassemble them in preparation for the next step—cutting the through-wedged mortise and tenon joints. Leave the pins proud for now. They will not be planed flush until the bench has been glued together.

If the legs haven't been cut to exact length yet, this is the time to cut them.

The assembled joint will be cleaned up after the bench components have been glued together.

CUTTING THE THROUGH-WEDGED MORTISE AND TENONS

I designed this bench with through-wedged mortise-and-tenon joints between the legs and the stretcher. A wedge spreads the end of a tenon to make it tighter in the mortise. Before reliable glues existed, dependable tenons had to be locked in place mechanically with pegs or wedges. These days, pegs and wedges are employed as much for appearance as for utility.

The process of cutting a through-wedged mortise and tenon is essentially the same as that used to cut a blind mortise and tenon (see pp. 102-115). The following instructions emphasize those parts of the process that differ.

The tools you will need to cut this joint include a mortising gauge, folding rule, knife, backsaw, square, ½-in. chisel, 1-in. or 1¼-in. chisel, mallet, drill, ⅜-in. or ⁷⁄₁₆-in. brad-point drill bits, sharp pencil and possibly a marking gauge or straightedge. The steps for cutting a through-wedged mortise and tenon are as follows:

1. MARK OUT THE MORTISE.

2. PARE BACK TO THE KNIFE LINES FROM WITHIN THE MORTISE.

3. DRILL OUT THE WASTE.

4. CHOP DOWN JUST SHY OF THE ENDS.

5. PARE THE MORTISE SIDES AND REMOVE THE WASTE.

6. CHOP THE ENDS TO THE KNIFE LINES.

7. PARE THE MORTISE SIDES AND ENDS SQUARE.

8. MARK THE TENON SHOULDERS AND LENGTH.

9. SCRIBE THE TENON THICKNESS.

10. MARK THE TENON WIDTH.

11. PARE BACK TO THE SHOULDERS.

12. SAW THE SHOULDERS WITH A BACKSAW.

13. SAW THE CHEEKS.

14. RE-MARK AND SAW THE WIDTH.

15. CLEAN UP AND FIT.

16. CUT THE WEDGE SLOTS.

17. MAKE THE WEDGES.

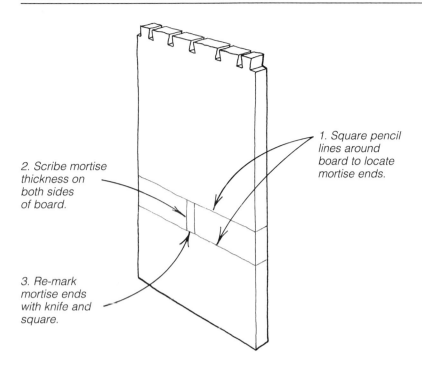

2. Scribe mortise thickness on both sides of board.

1. Square pencil lines around board to locate mortise ends.

3. Re-mark mortise ends with knife and square.

STEP 1.   MARK OUT THE MORTISE.

The through mortises must be accurately marked on both sides of each leg. Begin by squaring sharp pencil lines, 1¾ in. apart, around each board at the locations of the mortise ends. Then scribe the mortise thickness (½ in.), making sure you work from the same edge of each board when marking both sides. If you use a mortising gauge, save the setting between the pins to mark the tenons later. If your mortising gauge doesn't reach in far enough, you may be able to scribe the mortises with the marking gauge at two different settings. If neither gauge reaches, mark the mortises by carefully squaring fine pencil lines lengthwise around the legs.

Once the mortise thickness is established, re-mark the mortise ends on all sides with a knife and square.

STEP 2.   PARE BACK TO THE KNIFE LINES.

See p. 105.

STEP 3.   DRILL OUT THE WASTE.

The cautious approach is to drill halfway in from each side of the workpiece with a ⅜-in. or ⁷⁄₁₆-in. brad-point bit. Drilling all the way through from one side risks tearing out beyond the mortise sides when the bit pushes through. If you choose to drill through from one side, place the work on top of another piece of wood (or plywood) to keep the bit from coming through into empty space.

STEP 4.   CHOP DOWN JUST SHY OF THE ENDS.
Chop down about $\frac{1}{16}$ in. in from the mortise ends. Work from both sides to meet in the middle (see p. 106).

STEP 5.   PARE THE MORTISE SIDES AND REMOVE WASTE.
Gradually work your way down, from both sides, until the mortises are cleaned out. If you marked the mortise thickness with pencil lines, you may want to scribe over the line with an awl to provide a starting groove for the chisel.

STEP 6.   CHOP THE ENDS TO THE KNIFE LINES.
Chop the ends of the mortises at the knife lines, working down from both sides to meet in the middle (see p. 108).

STEP 7.   PARE THE MORTISE SIDES AND ENDS SQUARE.
The sides of the mortises should be flat. They are the edge-grain glue surfaces within the joint, and need to make close contact with the tenons. The mortise ends can be slightly back-cut inward toward the center.

STEP 8.   MARK THE TENON SHOULDERS AND LENGTH.
Hold the stretcher along the underside of the bench top. Since the stretcher has been left a little longer than necessary, it should project beyond both ends of the top. Use a knife to transfer the shoulder marks from the pins to the stretcher, thereby establishing the locations of the tenon shoulders on the stretcher. Square the tenon shoulders around all four sides of the stretcher with a knife.

Measure the desired tenon length out from each shoulder. A flush through tenon should be about $\frac{1}{16}$ in. proud until it is planed after glue-up. A proud tenon should be cut to finished length at this point. Since the stretcher is longer than necessary, square a line around each tenon end and cut off the excess.

STEP 9.   SCRIBE THE TENON THICKNESS.
If you scribed the mortise thickness with a mortising gauge, maintain the setting between the pins, but adjust the fence to center the tenon on the end of the stretcher.

If you laid out the mortise with a marking gauge or a pencil, set the mortising-gauge pins against the width of the actual mortise. Move the fence of the gauge to center the tenon on the stretcher.

STEP 10. MARK THE TENON WIDTH.
See p. 112. The tenons on this bench are 1¾ in. wide, centered between two ¼-in. shoulders.

STEP 11. PARE BACK TO THE SHOULDERS.
See p. 112.

STEP 12. SAW THE SHOULDERS WITH A BACKSAW.
See p. 112.

STEP 13. SAW THE CHEEKS.
See p. 114.

STEP 14. RE-MARK AND SAW THE WIDTH.
Saw the tenon width straight and true, since it will be visible in the assembled joint.

STEP 15. CLEAN UP AND FIT.
Fit the tenons to the mortises. They should mate perfectly on the cheeks. Any small gap at the ends will be taken up when the wedges are driven in.

STEP 16. CUT THE WEDGE SLOTS.
A wedge should spread a tenon against the end grain of the mortise. Pressure against the edge grain could split the wood that hosts the mortise. Make two saw kerfs across the widths of the tenons, no more than ¼ in. from each tenon edge, as shown in the photo on p. 146. Use a bandsaw or a thick-kerfed backsaw. A table-saw kerf is too wide.

RIGHT AND WRONG WAYS TO WEDGE A THROUGH TENON

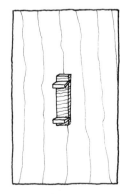

Right way: Wedges exert pressure against end grain of mortise.

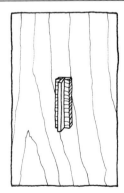

Wrong way: Wedge exerts pressure against edge grain of mortise.

Wedge kerfs are cut in the tenon to house the wedges, which are inserted when the joint is assembled.

STEP 17. MAKE THE WEDGES.

For color contrast, wedges are often made from a different wood than the rest of the piece. I chose walnut wedges for this cherry bench.

To make the wedges, mill a small piece of wood to the same thickness (½ in.) as the tenon, and cut narrow, thinly tapered wedges along the grain with a bandsaw or backsaw. Make sure the wedges are not so narrow that they bottom out in the kerf before spreading the wood. When you test-fit the joint, don't drive the wedges home—you would never get them out. Cut extra wedges in case you lose or break some in the hurry of gluing.

EDGE TREATMENT

Edges can be shaped in infinite variation, from the simplicity of a hard edge to the formality of a Roman ogee.

    The point in the furniture-making process at which an edge should be formed depends on the type of edge. A fancy routed edge would probably be done at this stage, between joining and surface preparation. The simple, broken edge (slightly rounded or chamfered) that our bench will have is more easily done after the piece has been glued together. (For a discussion of breaking the edges, see p. 156.)

SURFACE PREPARATION

Once the joinery has been cut, the bench is about halfway to completion. The remaining steps are surface preparation, gluing and finishing. The specific process I use to complete the project is as follows:

1. Remove all visible flaws with a hand scraper.
2. Sand with 120- or 150-grit sandpaper until the entire surface is evenly abraded.
3. Glue the piece together and let the glue dry overnight.
4. Clean up the joints.
5. Sand all as-yet-unsanded surfaces with 120- or 150-grit paper.
6. Break the edges.
7. Dampen the surface of the wood with water to raise the grain. Allow the wood to dry overnight.
8. Sand with 220-grit paper until all surfaces are smooth again.
9. Apply the finish.

    Where possible, surface preparation is done prior to gluing, while the components are still separate and easy to work with. Surface preparation involves scraping and sanding. The ideal wood surface has no dings, dips or tearout. Each successive use of sandpaper removes the coarser abrasions of the previous grit to make the surface finer and smoother. Though surface preparation can be the most tedious part of furniture making, patience and a watchful eye are rewarded. The more care you invest, the clearer and deeper the grain will appear when the finish is applied.

EDGE TREATMENTS

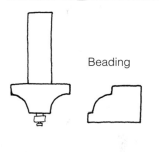

Hard edge

Chamfer

Quarter-round

ROUTED PROFILES

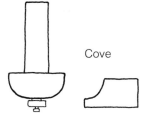

Beading

Cove

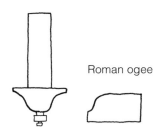

Roman ogee

Routed edges are cut with self-guiding bits—cutters that have bearings attached to limit their penetration. Edges can be molded on a router table or freehand.

To use the scraper, hold it upright with both hands and push it away from you along the grain of the board. If the scraper was sharpened correctly (see pp. 150-151), it should take a clean shaving.

SCRAPING

A hand scraper is a thin, rectangular piece of soft steel. A hooked burr, formed along the edge with a piece of harder steel, takes fine shavings without tearout, even when scraping against the grain.

The thickness of a scraper is important. If it's too thin, it will heat up quickly and burn your fingers. If it's too thick, it will lack the requisite flexibility. Scrapers made by Sandvik are among the best. They measure 0.80 millimeters thick by 2½ in. wide by 5⅞ in. long.

Preparing a scraper edge is an art in itself. Step-by-step instructions are given in the sidebar on pp. 150-151.

To use a scraper, hold it with the hook down and facing away from you. Grasp the ends with both hands, and place your thumbs in the middle to provide some flex. Push the scraper away from you, slightly flexed, along the grain. At an almost upright angle, the hook should bite and take a good shaving.

Scrapers do not stay sharp for long—instead of shavings they begin to make dust. You can resharpen several times by repeating steps 4 to 6 in the sidebar on pp. 150-151. After a while, though, you will want to put on a new edge, beginning with Step 1.

Scrape all the edge-grain surfaces of the bench, except in areas that will affect the fit of the joinery. Avoid the wood around each mortise where the tenon shoulders make contact. Similarly, avoid the pins and tails.

Scrape until all dings, plane marks and tearouts are gone. The surface should have an even quality. You can also scrape the end grain on the bottoms of the legs, but scraping end grain is more difficult. The scraper must be particularly sharp to handle end grain and tends to dig in along the edges. You may prefer to smooth the end grain with coarse sandpaper wrapped around a sanding block.

SANDING

Sand the scraped surfaces to a uniform degree of abrasion, again avoiding the joints. I usually go straight from the scraper to 150-grit sandpaper, but you may prefer 120 grit, especially if you haven't fully mastered the art of scraping.

Sand by hand or with an orbital sander. Belt sanders take off too much wood too fast, tend to leave ridges and can ruin a surface in a split second by rearing up on their back rollers to create a dip. Random orbital disc sanders also fail to offer the degree of control necessary for fine work.

An orbital sander has a felt-padded base that vibrates with an orbital motion. It removes wood more quickly than you can by hand, but in a more gradual and controlled manner than other power sanders. As long as an orbital sander is moved with the grain, the tiny swirls it creates become virtually invisible at the finer grits.

To sand by hand, wrap the sandpaper around a sanding block for greater efficiency, a flatter surface and reduced abrasion of your fingertips. You can purchase cork, foam or rubber-based sanding blocks, or make your own out of similar materials. Always sand with the grain. Cross-grain scratches are extremely visible and difficult to remove.

Sandpapers are classified according to the type and coarseness of the abrasive. Available grits range from 30 (extremely coarse) to 600 (very fine). The standard abrasive for wood, in grits up to 220, is open-coat aluminum oxide, which is tan colored. Another abrasive, silicon carbide, is used to make the black, wet/dry sandpaper used in the finishing process and for flattening sharpening stones, blade backs and plane bottoms.

When the scraped surfaces have been uniformly sanded with 120- or 150-grit open-coat aluminum oxide sandpaper, the bench is ready for assembly.

PREPARING A HAND SCRAPER

There are many variations on the basic method of preparing a scraper edge, and different degrees of perfection are suitable for different uses. For example, the coarse edge created by a file is great for removing paint and glue. A more polished edge leaves the surface smoother and is desirable in preparation for finishing.

Generally, only the two long edges of the scraper are "sharpened." First, they are flattened and squared with a file, and polished on stones. Then, they are formed into hooks with a burnisher.

With the scraper held firmly in the shoulder vise, file the edge with a mill bastard file.

Smooth the edges of the scraper on a medium-grit stone first (as shown) and then on a fine stone..

Polish the sides of the scraper on a fine stone.

The specific steps for preparing a hand scraper are as follows:
1. File the edge straight and square with a mill bastard file.
2. Hone the filed edge, first on a medium-grit stone, then on a fine stone. Hold the scraper perfectly upright to keep the edge square. Avoid wearing a groove in the stone.
3. Hone the sides with the scraper held flat on a fine stone.

4. Place the scraper on the bench top. Pull off any burr or hook with the burnisher held flat on top of the scraper. The burnisher is pulled along and off the edge in one motion.
5. Hold the scraper firmly on the bench top with its edge extending over the side. Stroke the edge with the burnisher held at 90°. Press hard. Imagine you are forcing the scraper edge upwards into a burr—the

burnisher moves over and up in one motion. Two or three hard strokes should do the trick.
6. Repeat the previous step with the burnisher held slightly (about 5°) off vertical. Imagine you are forming the burr you have just raised into a slight hook.

The scraper should now be ready to use. If it doesn't take clean shavings from wood, go back to Step 1 and work through the directions a second time.

Pull off the burr with a burnisher held flat on the scraper.

Stroke the edge of the scraper with the burnisher held at 90°. Then repeat with the burnisher at a slight angle (as shown).

BURNISHING A SCRAPER EDGE

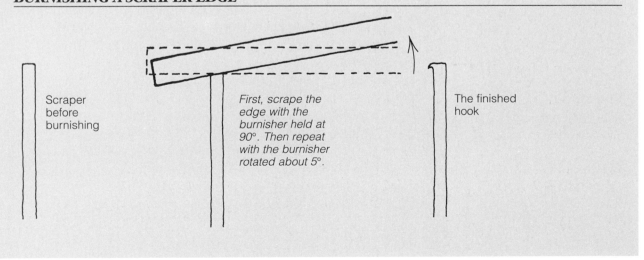

Scraper before burnishing

First, scrape the edge with the burnisher held at 90°. Then repeat with the burnisher rotated about 5°.

The finished hook

GLUING AND ASSEMBLY

There are many types of glue available, including white, yellow, plastic resin, hide, epoxy and casein. They vary in setting time, drying time, water resistance, ease of cleanup, color, toxicity, elasticity, durability and bonding characteristics.

The best general-purpose glue for woodworking is yellow (aliphatic-resin) glue. Sold under the names Titebond and Carpenter's Glue, aliphatic-resin glue is nontoxic, cleans up easily with water and provides a bond stronger than the internal one between wood fibers. It also has enough elasticity to adapt to a certain amount of wood movement over time—something more brittle glues can't cope with. I often dilute yellow glue so it will spread more easily by adding about 5% water. Yellow glue bonds best between wood surfaces that are in contact with one another. It doesn't fill gaps as well as epoxy and some other glues do.

For multiple laminations and other complex assemblies, a slower-setting glue such as plastic resin might be more appropriate. For outdoor furniture, where water resistance is a factor, there are a number of glues to choose from. Research to find the glue that fits your particular needs.

Gluing is the one part of furniture making where there is do-or-die time pressure. The second piece of furniture that I built was a rocking chair. I was too inexperienced to realize that I could glue it together in stages, so a friend and I tried to assemble the entire chair at one go. As we frantically pounded joints together and tightened clamps, the glue began to set. We redoubled our efforts, close to panic. Finally, everything was tightly together except the lowest stretcher between the back legs. The glue had set with one of the tenons only partially inserted, and neither clamping nor hammering would budge it. To this day, wherever that chair may be, there is still a ¼-in. gap at the tenon shoulder.

Preparation is the key to successful gluing. Always do a test run. Dry-clamp the bench without glue to be sure that every joint fits correctly, that the clamps are ready and that the necessary cauls are cut. (However, don't drive the wedges in until the actual glue-up).

A caul is a piece of wood used with clamps to direct their pressure and/or to protect the work from metal clamp jaws. For clamping the bench, a pair of special cauls should be cut to press the tails home around the pins. Another pair of cauls, with cutouts for the proud tenons, is required to press the mortise and tenons together.

Before glue-up, dry-clamp the bench with cauls in place to make sure that all the joints fit together correctly.

CAULS FOR GLUING THE BENCH

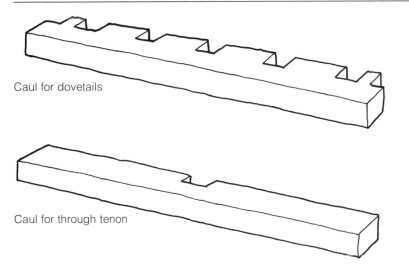

Caul for dovetails

Caul for through tenon

After dry-clamping successfully, gather the following materials in preparation for the actual glue-up:

- Glue. Some woodworkers apply glue from a squeeze bottle. I prefer to keep glue in a small, wide-mouthed jar and spread it with a brush.
- Brushes. A small, stiff brush is best for spreading glue in and around joints. I generally use the cheap "acid brushes" sold for plumbers at hardware stores. For edge gluing and laminations, where more glue needs to be spread, I recommend that you buy an inexpensive 1-in. paint brush and cut the bristles short for stiffness. A stiff 1-in. brush also works well for washing glue out of corners after assembly.
- A small bucket of warm water for washing glue off the wood and cleaning brushes.
- A white cotton rag for washing glue off the wood.
- A rubber mallet for knocking the joints together.
- A friend. An extra set of hands helps to spread glue quickly and to put on clamps and cauls.
- A hammer and wood block. Have a hammer on standby in case of emergency; you may need it to drive a joint home or break one apart. The wood block is to protect the furniture from hammer dents. In the case of our bench, a hammer is needed to drive the wedges into the tenon.

Spread glue quickly and evenly over both surfaces of every joint. If only one surface within a joint is coated, moisture is sucked up too quickly by the dry half, resulting in a weak, "glue-starved" joint.

Once the glue is spread, assemble the bench. Attach the top and stretcher to one of the legs, then put the other leg into place. Knock the joints together with the rubber mallet. Force them home with cauls and clamps. The cauls over the tenons should be placed to allow access to the wedge slots. Maintain even clamp pressure on both sides of the mortise to avoid damaging the leg or gluing it askew.

When the joints have been clamped so the shoulders pull up tight, spread glue on the wedges and drive them in with the hammer. If two wedges go into one tenon, as they do on our bench, insert them gradually and evenly. Alternate hammer taps from wedge to wedge. Otherwise the first one in will take up all the available space.

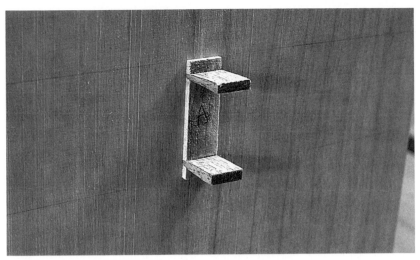

The wedged tenon will be trimmed flush once the glue has dried.

When the bench is fully assembled, make sure the legs are square to the bench top. The most likely problem is that excessive clamp pressure has bowed the top. If so, simply ease off on the clamps.

Wash off any visible glue with a brush and rag, especially where it has squeezed out of interior corners. Leave the clamps on for at least one hour. Let the glue dry overnight before going on to the next step.

CLEANING UP THE JOINTS

Through tenons can be left proud or planed flush. Begin by sawing off the protruding wedges with a backsaw. If the tenons are to be proud, smooth the ends with a block plane or file, followed by a sanding block. If the tenons are to be flush, take them down completely with a block plane, then scrape and sand the surface as you did the rest of the bench. Similarly, the protruding pins of the dovetail joints should be planed or filed flush, then scraped and sanded.

When planing end grain, there is a danger that the edges will splinter off as the blade leaves the wood. Paring a bevel along the edges solves the problem and makes a nice detail. To prevent edge-splintering from extending below the surface of the joint as you plane it flush, score the base of protruding parts with a knife. They will break cleanly at the knife cut.

If the sides of the legs are not already flush with the sides of the top, plane them flush with the block plane or a bench plane.

Once the joints, edges and corners are cleaned up, sand them with 120- or 150-grit paper—whichever you used on the rest of the bench. Also sand any other unsanded parts near joints. To sand interior corners, fold small sheets of sandpaper in half and use them by hand.

BREAKING THE EDGES

The choice of edge treatment (see p. 147) should fit the use and aesthetic intent of a piece of furniture. A heavily rounded edge is user friendly, but can seem informal to the point of slovenliness. A molded edge is often reminiscent of antique furniture. A sharp edge is formal and gives maximum definition to the lines of a design. In general, a crisper edge reveals more exacting craftsmanship.

For this bench, I prefer a slightly broken edge made with 120-grit paper and a sanding block. The edge can be chamfered or rounded. My intention is to have crisp lines without the coldness of a totally hard edge. Break the edges of your bench to the extent you desire. If sandpaper doesn't take off as much wood as you like, begin with a file.

WETTING THE SURFACE

At this point, the bench is fully formed in every detail, and all surfaces have been sanded with either 120- or 150-grit paper.

The abrasive action of sandpaper cuts off some fibers but crushes others down. Dampening the surface causes the crushed fibers to swell, making them more vulnerable to the next sanding, much like those advertisements in which shaving cream made whiskers stand up.

Apply water to all surfaces of the bench with a rag, dampening the wood but not flooding it. Let the bench dry overnight.

FINAL SANDING

Sand the entire bench with 220-grit paper. Sand with the grain and into corners as much as possible. An orbital sander will reach most of the surfaces, or you can do the entire job by hand. When sanding is complete, the bench is ready for finishing.

APPLYING THE FINISH

Finishes protect wood against dirt and liquids, provide a partial moisture barrier and enhance wood's appearance. Of the many types of finish available (see the sidebar on pp. 157-159), my favorite is an oil/varnish mixture, which combines some of the good points of each component. I prefer to mix my own formula rather than use one of the commercially available mixes. (You can experiment by developing your own mixture with whatever oils and varnishes are available.)

FINISHES AND FILLERS

There are many finishes, each of which has strengths and weaknesses. They vary in ease of application, water resistance, solvent resistance, dirt resistance, surface buildup, gloss, durability, toxicity and ease of repair. The most commonly used finishes are oils, varnish and urethane, oil/varnish mixtures, wax, wiping varnishes, shellac and lacquers.

OILS

Two types of oil are used for finishing furniture: linseed oil, which is pressed from flax seed, and tung oil (also known as china wood oil), which comes from the nut of the tung tree. Though tung oil originated in China, much of it is now exported from South America. Tung oil is superior to linseed oil, with greater water resistance and less tendency to yellow over time.

In their pure forms, these oils dry slowly and stay relatively soft. To make them dry faster and harder, they are often treated with heat and/or additives in the manufacturing process. Treated linseed oil is called "boiled" linseed oil.

The advantages of oil finishes are:
- Ease of application. You just put some oil on the wood with a rag, let it soak in and wipe off the excess.
- Appearance. Properly applied oil finishes dry in the wood, rather than on top of it. The absence of surface buildup gives the wood a visual and tactile immediacy that most other finishes lack.
- Ease of repair. Stains and scratches can be sanded out and re-oiled without stripping the entire surface. However, on woods that change color because of oxidation or exposure to sunlight, a freshly sanded spot will stay a different color for quite a while.

The disadvantages of oil finishes are:
- Relatively little protection against liquids, moisture and scratches.
- Many coats are required to develop a decent buildup.
- Wet oil can bleed out of the pores for hours. Unless you stay on hand to wipe the surface, bleed-out dries into shiny little spots.

VARNISH AND URETHANE

Varnishes are surface coatings, traditionally made by cooking oil and resin together and combining the mixture with thinner (mineral spirits). Modern varnishes usually substitute synthetic alkyd resin for natural resins. Urethane is very similar to varnish, except that it contains some proportion of polyurethane resin.

Varnish is applied with a brush, dries much harder than oil and takes a long time to dry. Excellent resistance to water, solvents and moisture, as well as abrasion protection, makes varnish an ideal finish for marine and outdoor uses. On fine furniture, however, varnish creates too thick a surface film for my taste—the wood looks as though it is sealed in plastic.

Practice and care are required in applying varnish, which readily shows brush marks, traps air bubbles and picks up dust.

OIL/VARNISH MIXTURES

Oil/varnish mixtures are applied like oil, but dry faster and harder, with fewer coats required to build up a good-looking finish. There is no appreciable surface coating to destroy the tactile quality of the wood. Although they are nowhere near as protective as thick coats of straight varnish, oil/varnish mixtures definitely provide better moisture and liquid resistance than does oil alone.

Oil/varnish mixtures are at their greatest disadvantage as tabletop finishes, because standing water penetrates them. The result can be discoloration of the finish and/or discoloration and change of texture in the wood. Water stains can often be repaired by rubbing with fine steel wool or wet sanding with more finish.

I use oil/varnish mixtures on tabletops, anyway. The wonderful appearance more than offsets the maintenance risks. A more protective finish would necessarily take the form of a thicker surface coating.

WAX

Wax is generally used as a coating over other finishes, rather than as a primary finish. It does not provide much protection, but can greatly enhance appearance.

Common waxes used on furniture include paraffin, carnauba and beeswax. Most commercially sold paste-wax finishes include one or more of these waxes, mixed with solvent to make them soft enough for easy application.

I do not put wax on my furniture. It is a high-maintenance finish that requires frequent repolishing. Just the warmth of a person's hand can soften wax enough to disrupt the surface, and when water penetrates wax it often discolors the wood underneath.

WIPING VARNISHES

Many of the "oil" and "tung oil" products sold to woodworkers these days are actually wiping varnishes—varnishes that have been thinned with a high proportion of mineral spirits. Moreover, some "tung oil" products don't contain any tung oil.

Wiping varnishes are applied like oil finishes, but dry as thin surface coatings. Since very many applications would be required to build up a sufficient depth of finish to allow the shiny surface to be buffed out evenly, a thin varnish coating tends to look streaky and cheap.

SHELLAC

Shellac is made from a secretion of the lac beetle. It originated in the Orient and was long the premier finish for fine European furniture, but has generally been replaced by more durable synthetic lacquers.

Shellac is brittle (as are varnish and lacquer). The fine crackling we associate with antiques is shellac's response to the seasonal movement of wood. Shellac is also quickly damaged by water or alcohol.

Natural shellac has an orange tint that some furniture makers feel favorably warms up the appearance of dark woods. "Blond" shellac has been bleached clear and can be used on any wood.

Shellac is sold as dry flakes or premixed with alcohol. In liquid form, shellac has a shorlt shelf life: it loses the ability to dry hard. Check the expiration date on the can when you buy premixed shellac (it can often be found under the price sticker). Making your own mixture from shellac flakes and alcohol avoids waste; you can mix just as much as you need.

With alcohol for a solvent, thin coats of shellac dry almost instantaneously. A technique known as "French polishing" takes advantage of this characteristic to build up a complete, lustrous finish in one sustained onslaught. A cotton rag, enclosing a wad of cotton material charged with shellac, is rubbed over wood with a continuous motion. As shellac builds up on the wood, drops of linseed oil are applied to offset the increased drag on the pad. The process concludes with long sweeps along the grain from end to end to avoid stop/start marks.

Shellac can also be applied with a brush. It is sometimes used as an initial sealer prior to other finishing processes.

LACQUERS

"Lacquer" describes a broad family of synthetic finishes. These include more traditional nitrocellulose-based lacquers and the new water-based lacquers. Lacquer is generally applied with spray guns. So-called "padding lacquer" is really shellac.

Like varnish and shellac, lacquer is a surface finish. The popularity of lacquer among professional furniture makers and manufacturers stems from the speed and control with which it can be applied, its relative hardness and the ease with which gloss and tint can be varied.

FILLERS

The pores of open-grained woods such as oak and mahogany tend to telegraph through a surface finish, especially in reflected light. Unless the pores are filled ahead of time, many layers of finish must be applied and sanded flat to fill them before surface buildup can begin.

Fillers are fine-grained pastes or powders that can be tinted to match the wood. They are used to fill open pores before applying finish. Traditionally, plaster of Paris was used to fill mahogany before French polishing. Nowadays, paste fillers are made from silica that has been mixed with a binder of varnish or oil and thinned with naphtha.

Filler is unnecessary when using an oil or oil/varnish mixture, since there is no surface buildup to highlight pores.

The recipe for my finish is one-third pure tung oil, one-third Waterlox Transparent (a brand of semi-gloss wiping varnish made from tung oil) and one-third mineral spirits. I allow the mixture to sit overnight in a sealed jar to give the ingredients time to mix. The setting time of the mixture can be slowed by increasing the proportion of pure tung oil, or speeded up with more Waterlox.

Only three coats of my oil/varnish formula are required to build up a good finish. If you choose to finish your bench with it, the steps are as follows; if you make your own oil/varnish finish, the same steps apply, but you might need more coats.

STEP 1

When the bench has been finish-sanded with 220-grit paper, dust it off with an air hose and/or rags. Apply the first coat of finish with a small, clean, cotton rag. Cover all surfaces liberally, and keep them wet for five or ten minutes so plenty of oil can soak in. Wipe the surface dry with cotton rags before the finish gets tacky.

There may be some bleed-out, but it won't last more than half an hour. Give the bench a rubdown every five or ten minutes during that half hour. Let the bench dry overnight before going on to Step 2.

On large pieces of furniture, it is often advisable to oil and dry one section at a time to prevent the oil from setting up before there is time to wipe it off.

STEP 2

With a rag, apply the second coat of finish to one area of the bench at a time, such as the stretcher or the inside of a leg. Lightly sand the wet surfaces with 400-grit wet/dry sandpaper, moving with the grain. The intent is to smooth the surface, not to remove wood. Before the oil sets, wipe the surface dry and move on to another section of the bench.

When the entire bench has been wet-sanded in this manner, rub it down several more times with dry cotton rags to prevent bleed-out. Pay special attention to interior corners, where oil is likely to collect.

Let the bench dry overnight before applying the final coat.

STEP 3

Repeat Step 2 with 600-grit wet/dry sandpaper. Let the bench dry overnight.

The next day, examine the bench top in reflected light. It may look streaky as a result of uneven wet sanding. If so, try buffing the top under hard pressure with a clean rag. If it still looks streaky, lightly buff the entire surface with 0000 steel wool, followed by a cotton rag, moving with the grain.

The completed bench.

Congratulations! The bench is now complete. Take it in the house and use it. Even if all the details aren't perfect, your bench is likely to be around for a lot longer than you and I. As with all fine furniture, it is best to keep it out of direct sunlight, which will bleach the wood. Likewise, avoid prolonged contact with water.

Now that you have made a piece of furniture from start to finish, it should be evident that good-quality work builds step by step. The attention given to each detail affects the integrity of the whole. With practice, your hands will come to understand the tools and your eyes will learn to discern the details that add up to successful results. Practice makes perfect, so let's move on to the next project.

PROJECT 5:

BUILDING A
WALL CABINET

Our final project expands upon skills developed in the previous four projects by introducing techniques such as drawer making, frame-and-panel construction and routing a tongue-and-groove joint.

The design is a variation upon a traditional British teaching project: a wall-hung cabinet with one drawer and a frame-and-panel door. The option of adjustable shelving gives the cabinet functional flexibility.

A relatively complex project like this is best approached one stage at a time. First, we'll construct the carcase (pp. 165-176), then build the drawer to fit (pp. 177-181) and, finally, make and mount the door (pp. 182-188). Each stage is comprehensible on its own. Rather than be repetitive, instructions are based on the assumption that the reader has read and completed the previous projects.

The scale plans given in the bottom drawing on p. 164 are more complex than those I would draw for myself. By necessity of the book format, they attempt to contain the complete information that would normally be included in a full-scale drawing. Feel free to alter dimensions and to draw your own full-scale plans. Substitute half-blind dovetails for through dovetails wherever you choose.

WALL CABINET

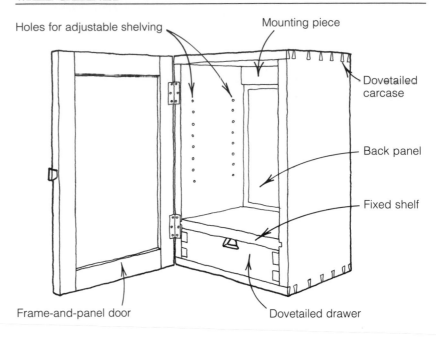

Holes for adjustable shelving

Mounting piece

Dovetailed carcase

Back panel

Fixed shelf

Frame-and-panel door

Dovetailed drawer

SCALE DRAWING OF WALL CABINET

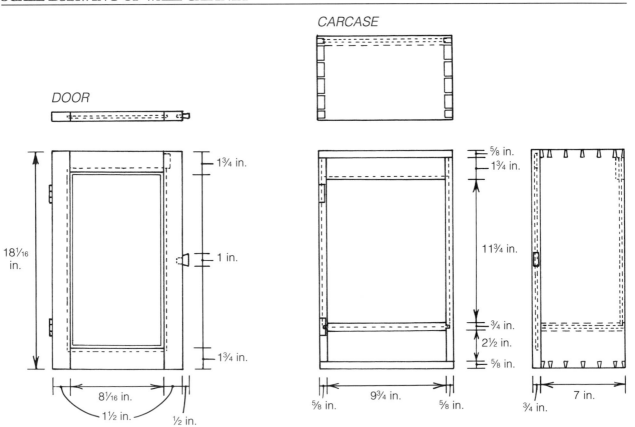

CARCASE

DOOR

18¹⁄₁₆ in.

1¾ in.

1 in.

1¾ in.

8¹⁄₁₆ in.

1½ in.

½ in.

⅝ in.

1¾ in.

11¾ in.

¾ in.

2½ in.

⅝ in.

⅝ in.

9¾ in.

⅝ in.

¾ in.

7 in.

BUILDING THE CARCASE

The carcase of the cabinet is a dovetailed box with a shelf and a mounting piece across the interior. The back of the carcase is a ⅜-in. thick panel that slips into a ¼-in. groove. The steps for building the carcase are as follows:

1. MAKE A CUTTING LIST.

2. SELECT THE LUMBER.

3. MILL THE WOOD.

4. DOVETAIL THE CARCASE TOGETHER.

5. CUT THE GROOVES.

6. CUT THE TONGUES.

7. FIT THE PANEL.

8. DRILL HOLES FOR ADJUSTABLE SHELVING.

9. SCRAPE AND SAND.

10. GLUE THE CARCASE TOGETHER.

11. CLEAN UP THE OUTSIDE.

- 2 pieces at ⅝ in. x 7 in. x 18⅛ in. (the sides, including ¹⁄₁₆-in. waste at each end)

- 2 pieces at ⅝ in. x 7 in. x 11⅛ in. (the top and bottom, including ¹⁄₁₆-in. waste at each end)

- 1 piece at ¾ in. x 7 in. x 10⅜ in. (the shelf)

- 1 piece at ¾ in. x 1¾ in. x 10⅜ in. (the mounting piece)

- 1 piece at ⅜ in. x 10¼ in. x 12¼ in. (the back panel)

STEP 1. MAKE A CUTTING LIST.

If you intend to follow the plans in the scale drawing on p. 164 exactly, the cutting list for the carcase is as shown at left. The final measurements of the shelf, mounting piece and back panel will be taken from the exact dimensions of the actual carcase during construction. In the meantime, leave the shelf and mounting piece a little longer than indicated on the cutting list. Leave the panel both longer and wider, about ¼ in. in each dimension.

STEP 2. SELECT THE LUMBER.

I prefer to find one board from which I can take the entire cabinet, including the drawer and the door, so that grain and color match throughout. Resawing a thick board is one way to get a lot of wood out of a single timber. The cabinet in the photographs began as a plank of 8/4 cherry.

STEP 3. MILL THE WOOD.

If you start with 8/4 lumber, resaw pieces of it in half to get the rough blanks for the ⅝-in. and ¾-in. thick components. The pieces for the ⅜-in. thick panel can be roughed out by sawing 8/4 lumber into thirds.

Resaw on a bandsaw, either freehand or with a fence set for drift (see p. 44). To prepare a board for freehand bandsawing, first make the bottom edge square to one of the sides. That way, the board will sit vertically on the bandsaw table. Then mark the desired cut on the top edge with a pencil and straightedge. Always resaw wood thicker than the finished thickness you intend to arrive at, to allow for wood movement as tension is released. For example, if the finished thickness of the boards is to be ⅝ in., resaw to at least ¾ in. Let resawn lumber sit for a day or two before continuing the milling process so that any changes in the board's internal stress can reach equilibrium.

The author resaws a piece of 8/4 cherry for the carcase of the cabinet.

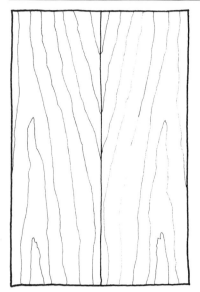

Bookmatching can create appealing grain configurations.

Whether you begin with 8/4 or 4/4 lumber, mill the wood four-square to the specifications of your cutting list, allowing extra length or width as suggested in Step 1. At the same time, mill a few extra pieces to the same thickness and length as the shelf and mounting piece (perhaps out of a less expensive wood); you will use these pieces to test machine setups when cutting the tongues. (For detailed directions on milling a board four-square, see pp. 83-99.)

If the back panel will be made from two edge-glued boards, resawing offers the opportunity for bookmatching, in which two faces that have been sawn apart are assembled edge to edge as mirror images of each other. The resulting pattern can be striking.

There are two approaches to assembling a panel. One is to mill the pieces of wood to final thickness before gluing them together. The other is to glue thicker pieces together, then plane the full panel to ⅜ in.

STEP 4.   DOVETAIL THE CARCASE TOGETHER.

The tails are laid out on the sides of the cabinet, rather than on the top and bottom. This configuration ensures that they will be visible when the cabinet is hung. Also, with tails on the sides, the mechanical strength of the joint counters gravity. With pins on the sides, only glue strength would oppose gravity.

Lay out the dovetails in a pattern you find pleasing; cut them as described on pp. 119-125. If you prefer to use half-blind dovetails, follow the directions on pp. 135-141. After marking the tail-shoulder locations on one cabinet side, transfer the marks directly to the other cabinet side, so that both sides end up exactly the same length. Do the same for the pin shoulders on the top and bottom of the carcase.

When the dovetails fit together, dry-assemble the carcase (without glue) and hand-plane the front and back edges flush in preparation for cutting the grooves. Then disassemble before cutting the grooves.

STEP 5.   CUT THE GROOVES.

The grooves for the shelf, back panel and mounting piece measure ¼ in. wide by ⁵⁄₁₆ in. deep. The grooves for the shelf can be cut with a table saw or a router. The stopped grooves for the back panel and mounting piece are more effectively made with a router.

Before making the grooves, mark their locations clearly enough to be sure you don't cut them in the wrong places. The lower end of the panel groove in the cabinet sides will stop about ⅜ in. beyond its intersection with the shelf. The upper end can stop just a hair beyond the inside of the carcase top.

DETAIL OF TONGUE-AND-GROOVE JOINT

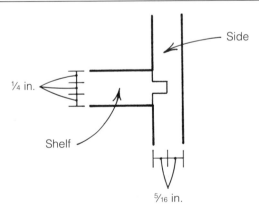

¼ in.

Side

Shelf

⁵⁄₁₆ in.

The ¼-in. groove for the shelf can be cut on the table saw, using a miter gauge with a stop attached to the fence.

To cut the shelf grooves on the table saw:
Table-saw grooves are best cut with a dado blade, though they can also be made by repeated passes with a single blade. Assuming you have a dado blade, assemble it to ¼-in. thickness. If it is the better type, consisting of separate blades, be sure that the teeth rake outward to either side. Crank the blade about ⁵⁄₁₆ in. above the table for the desired depth of cut.

Push the wood over the blade with a miter gauge that has been set square or with a sliding table used for dadoes. Greater accuracy will result if a stop is clamped to the fence on the miter guide or sliding table to position the workpiece. Take a sample cut on a scrap piece to check the settings before making the actual grooves.

To cut the shelf groove with a router, run the router against a clamped fence.

To cut the shelf grooves with a router:

Install a ¼-in. diameter straight bit in the router. Accurately mark the locations of the grooves on the cabinet sides with a pencil. Then square a line across each piece, at the same distance from the groove as the bit is from the outside edge of the router base. Clamp a piece of wood along the line to serve as a fence.

To rout the grooves, slide the router base firmly against the fence. Make sure the workpiece is held securely in place, so it won't move while being routed. To avoid overstressing the bit, make a first pass about ³⁄₁₆ in. deep and a second pass at the final depth of ⁵⁄₁₆ in. For both grooves to come out at the exact same depth, the two sides should be routed in parallel steps: fences clamped on both, the first pass on both and then the final pass on both.

To cut the panel grooves with a router:

Install a ¼-in. diameter straight bit in the router. Set a fence on the router or router table ¼ in. away from the bit, which is the distance the panel groove sets in from the back of the carcase. Make successively deeper passes to avoid straining the bit, rather than one pass ⁵⁄₁₆ in. deep. Take test cuts on a scrap piece to check the settings.

Rout the grooves with the fence firmly against the workpiece. For the stopped grooves in the cabinet sides, the best method is to work freehand with a plunge router that can be lowered into the wood at the start of the cut and raised at completion. With a standard router that doesn't plunge, simply lower and lift the entire machine while it is running.

On a router table, begin the stopped grooves by laying the wood down on the spinning cutter. Maintain firm control and keep the work against the fence at all times to prevent the bit from grabbing the wood. Before starting, draw a pair of lines up the face of the fence to indicate the bit's position, and another pair of lines around the workpiece at the locations where the grooves should end. The correspondence of the lines indicates where to start and stop the spinning bit, which is otherwise hidden in the groove. End the cut by lifting the wood off the table.

The panel grooves in the top of the shelf and the bottom of the mounting piece are taken all the way through to the ends.

STEP 6.   CUT THE TONGUES.

A tongue should fit a groove much as a tenon fits a mortise—snug but not too tight. Before making the tongues on the ends of the shelf and mounting piece, cut their ends square and to final length, which is the distance between the cabinet sides, plus the combined depth of the grooves. (Cut the test pieces milled earlier to the same length.) The distance between the sides can be measured between the pin shoulders on the top or bottom of the carcase. The depth of the grooves is most accurately taken by holding them face to face to measure their combined depth.

Tongues can be cut with a table saw or a router. One standard approach for each machine is given below. Test pieces should be used to verify machine settings.

To cut the tongues on a table saw:

The tongues on the shelf and mounting piece are centered, so shoulders are sawn from both faces of the board. When sawing the shoulders, place the workpiece flat on the table, with the end to be joined butted against the rip fence. Push the work through with a miter gauge to avoid kickback. Set the blade height to a hair under the shoulder depth (about ¼ in.). The distance from the rip fence to the far side of the sawblade establishes the length of the tongue (about 5/16 in. in this case).

Take cuts on both ends of a test piece first to make sure the shoulders will end up the right distance apart and to check the blade height. When the test piece comes out right, make the shoulders on the actual boards.

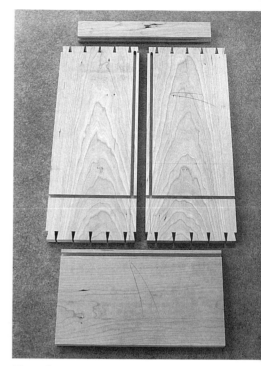

The cabinet mounting piece, sides and shelf with grooves cut.

There are two different ways to saw the cheeks on the table saw. In one method, the fence is kept in a constant position and the board is flipped over to saw the second cheek. With this flip-over method, the tongue comes out perfectly centered. The disadvantage is that tongues sawn in succession will not come out at identical thicknesses if a board is thinner at one end because of snipe (see p. 44-45).

In the second method, both cheeks are cut with the same board face against the rip fence. After all the tongues have their first cheek cut, the rip fence is readjusted to saw the second cheek. This way, the tongues on multiple pieces always come out identically thick, though perhaps not perfectly centered.

Whichever method you use, test the settings on a scrap piece that already has shoulders cut on it, to make sure the tongue fits the groove snugly. On the mounting piece, the tongue should line up perfectly with the panel groove cut in Step 5.

To saw the cheeks, set the blade height to just a hair less than the tongue length. Use a push stick to hold the wood (tongue down) firmly against the fence and to move it along. Attach a high auxiliary fence to your standard rip fence for added control and safety.

To cut the tongues on the shelf with a table saw, attach a high auxiliary fence to the rip fence for greater control and safety.

To cut the tongues with a router:

Install a wide, straight bit in the router, ½ in. or more in diameter. Set a fence on the router table to limit the bit's penetration to the intended tongue length. The height of the bit determines the thickness of the tongue, which will be what remains after shoulders are routed on both sides of the board. Rout a test piece to make sure the shoulders come out the right distance apart and to check the thickness of the tongue. There are three alternative ways to make a tongue fit well:

- Cut sample tongues on scraps that are the same thickness as the shelf and mounting piece. Adjust the bit height until the tongues fit the grooves perfectly.
- Make the actual tongue a little thick and gradually raise the router bit for successive passes.
- Make the actual tongue a little thick and fit it with a rabbet plane.

Slide the end of the work along the fence. If you are running the end of a narrow piece of wood against the fence, a square push block increases safety and accuracy. If you are routing freehand, clamp the shelf down and move the router's edge guide along the end of the work.

The tongue should line up with the panel groove that has already been cut in the mounting piece.

The tongue on the end of the mounting piece can be made on a router table. The square push block keeps the narrow mounting piece steady as it passes the cutter.

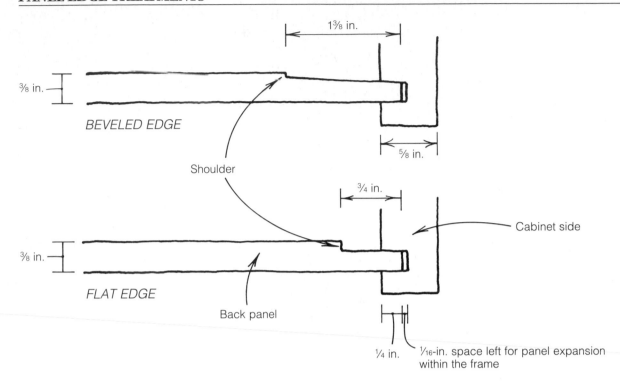

3⁄8 in.

1³⁄8 in.

BEVELED EDGE

5⁄8 in.

Shoulder

3⁄4 in.

Cabinet side

3⁄8 in.

FLAT EDGE

Back panel

¼ in. ¹⁄16-in. space left for panel expansion within the frame

STEP 7. **FIT THE PANEL.**

Cut the panel to its final dimensions. The overall width of the panel should allow about ⅛-in. total clearance for expansion in the grooves.

The ⅜-in. thick panel has to fit into ¼-in. grooves. There are several options for thinning the panel edges. Most commonly, a flat or beveled edge comes to a shoulder, as shown in the drawing above. Either version can be cut on a table saw, much as a tongue is cut. Generally, the shoulder is sawn first, the thickness, second. However, when the shoulder is less than a sawblade-thickness deep, only the thickness needs to be cut—the height of the blade will create the shoulder.

The shoulders should be set back far enough to prevent them from pushing against the frame when the panel expands. Make whichever panel design you prefer. I like the straightforwardness of a flat edge for this cabinet.

To cut a beveled edge on the panel, change the angle of the sawblade to a slight taper. Too radical a taper doesn't work: if the panel shrinks, gaps show; if it expands, the steep angle pushes against

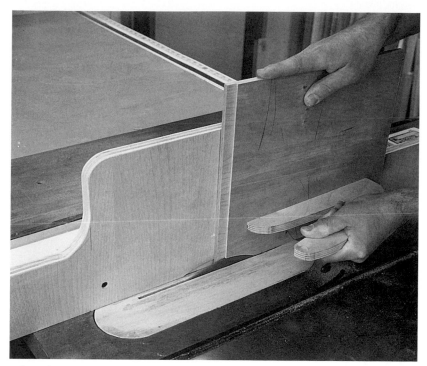

When thinning the panel edge, use a modified push stick to hold the panel flat against the auxiliary fence.

Drill holes for the adjustable shelf supports.

the frame. If your table saw's blade tilts toward the fence, rather than away from it, you'll have to move the fence to the other side of the blade to make the cut. Test the settings on a scrap piece. Final fitting can be done with a hand plane.

STEP 8. DRILL HOLES FOR ADJUSTABLE SHELVING.

Adjustable shelf supports can be bought or made. If you plan to buy them, do so ahead of time, or at least be certain you know the diameter and depth of the required holes.

Mark the hole locations on one side of the carcase. (Mine are placed 1 in. from the front and back of the shelf. They are unobtrusive, but far enough apart to give the shelf stability.) Square the marks over to the other side piece to be sure they line up exactly. Drill the holes with a drill press or hand drill. Use a depth stop to avoid drilling through to the outside of the cabinet. The adjustable shelves for the cabinet will be made at a later stage (see p. 193).

Glue the carcase together, using clamps and cauls.

STEP 9. SCRAPE AND SAND.

It is much easier to sand the carcase interior before assembly. Scrape and sand (with 120- or 150-grit paper) all surfaces that will be on the interior, and both sides of the panel. Don't touch the areas that form the joints. (For a detailed discussion of scraping and sanding, see pp. 147-149.)

STEP 10. GLUE THE CARCASE TOGETHER.

Dry-clamp the entire carcase, including the panel, shelf and mounting piece. Make sure that all joints pull tightly together and that the mounting piece sits snugly up against the cabinet top. If everything fits, glue the carcase together for real (see pp. 152-155 for a detailed discussion of the gluing process). Be sure to check the carcase for squareness before the glue dries.

  Remember, the panel should remain free-floating to allow for shrinkage and expansion, so don't put glue in the grooves that hold it. Many furniture makers prefinish panels before gluing; this prevents glue from sticking to them and makes applying finish to the completed cabinet easier later on.

STEP 11. CLEAN UP THE OUTSIDE.

Let the glue dry overnight. Then plane or file the joints flush at each corner.

BUILDING THE DRAWER

You probably won't be surprised to learn that there are many ways of making drawers. One sequence that works for me is as follows:

1. MAKE A CUTTING LIST.

2. SELECT AND MILL THE LUMBER.

3. FIT THE DRAWER FRONT TO THE OPENING.

4. MARK AND SAW THE DOVETAILS.

5. CUT THE BOTTOM GROOVE.

6. FIT THE BOTTOM.

7. MAKE THE FINGER PULL.

8. SCRAPE AND SAND.

9. GLUE THE DRAWER TOGETHER.

10. PLANE TO FIT.

11. GLUE IN A STOP.

SCALE DRAWING OF DRAWER

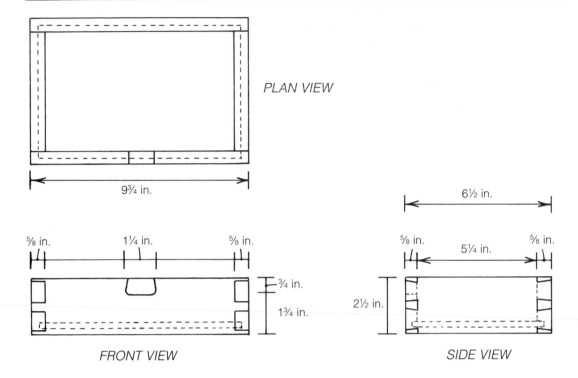

PLAN VIEW

9¾ in.

⅝ in.   1¼ in.   ⅝ in.

¾ in.

1¾ in.

FRONT VIEW

6½ in.

⅝ in.   5¼ in.   ⅝ in.

2½ in.

SIDE VIEW

<table>
<tr><td>

CUTTING LIST FOR DRAWER

- 2 pieces at ⅝ in. x 2½ in. x 9¾ in. (the front and back)

- 2 pieces at ⅝ in. x 2½ in. x 6⅝ in. (the sides, with ¹⁄₁₆-in. waste at each end)

- 1 piece at ¼ in. x 5¾ in. x 9 in. (the bottom panel)

</td></tr>
</table>

STEP 1.   MAKE A CUTTING LIST.

Take the drawer's measurements from the opening in the carcase. The length of the drawer should be about ½ in. less than the depth of the opening, to leave room for a stop at the back. If the measurements of the drawer opening were exactly true to the drawing on p. 164, the cutting list would be as shown at left.

STEP 2.   SELECT AND MILL THE LUMBER.

To end up with a snug fit, drawer components are initially milled to the full width of the drawer opening. They will be planed to fit after assembly. Leave some extra length on all parts until the front is fit to the opening and the joints are marked out.

I used cherry throughout my cabinet, including the drawer, but you may want to conserve your best wood by making only the front of the drawer in the same species as the cabinet carcase. The sides, back and bottom can be made from a less precious species.

The drawer front should be cut to fit the opening tightly.

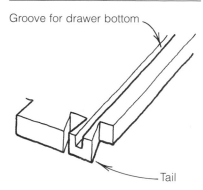

Groove for drawer bottom

Tail

Generally, dovetails should be laid out so that the groove for the drawer bottom runs through the last tail. The groove can be cut completely through a half-blind dovetail (as shown). In a through dovetail, the groove should stop before the end to keep it from showing.

STEP 3.   FIT THE DRAWER FRONT TO THE OPENING.

Cut the drawer front to fit the opening so tightly, in length and width, that it would be stuck if you put it in all the way.

STEP 4.   MARK AND SAW THE DOVETAILS.

In this method of drawer construction, the pin shoulders are marked in from each end of the drawer front to accept the exact thickness of the sides. Unlike the dovetails we cut in projects 3 and 4, these dovetails do not have proud pins. This method ensures that the drawer sides will be flush with the front, which already fits the drawer opening snugly. After assembly, the sides will be planed down to allow the drawer to slide in and out freely. Once the shoulders are laid out on the drawer front, transfer the marks to the drawer back.

The layout of the dovetails should take into account the location of the groove for the drawer bottom. Construction is simpler if the groove is centered through the last tail, avoiding the pins entirely (see the drawing above). If the drawer is made with half-blind dovetails, the groove can be cut completely through the drawer sides, front and back and remain invisible from the outside. For through dovetails, a stopped groove is made in the drawer sides (the tailboards) and a through groove in the drawer front and back.

After the dovetails are cut and fit, dry-assemble the drawer and plane its bottom edges flush with one another.

The drawer components with dovetails and grooves cut.

STEP 5.   CUT THE BOTTOM GROOVE.

The grooves for the drawer bottom are drawn to be ¼ in. wide by
⁵⁄₁₆ in. deep. If there are through dovetails at the front , rout a stopped
groove in the drawer sides, as seen in the photo above. Register the
fence against the bottom edges of the drawer components, which
are already flush with one another.

STEP 6.   FIT THE BOTTOM.

For a small drawer like this, a ¼-in. thick bottom is quite strong
enough. Although this cabinet calls for solid wood throughout, I have
often used veneered plywood for drawer bottoms and cabinet backs.
Plywood works well for panels because it is more dimensionally
stable than solid timber.

   Cut the drawer bottom to fit. There should be room around the
sides for expansion—a solid-wood panel like this could vary in width
between ¹⁄₁₆ in. and ⅛ in. over the course of a year.

STEP 7.   MAKE THE FINGER PULL.

Mark and cut a finger pull in the drawer front. The pull can be any
shape, as long as it is large enough for the tip of an index finger. The
design in the drawings is intended to echo the shape of the dovetails,
since they are such a prominent feature of the cabinet.

The assembled drawer with joints planed flush and sanded.

STEP 8. SCRAPE AND SAND.

Scrape and sand the interiors of the drawer components and both sides of the bottom panel. Stay away from the joints. (For a detailed discussion of scraping and sanding, see pp. 147-149.)

STEP 9. GLUE THE DRAWER TOGETHER.

Dry-clamp and then glue the drawer together, making sure to check for squareness before the glue dries. (For a detailed discussion of gluing and assembly, see pp. 152-155.)

STEP 10. PLANE TO FIT.

Plane the joints flush at the corners of the drawer. Then fit the drawer into the opening by gradually planing the sides and edges, as needed. At the most humid time of year, the drawer should ride freely in and out of the opening, yet fit without play from side to side or up and down. If you are working in the winter, when the indoor humidity drops as a result of heating, you may want to allow some play for seasonal expansion.

STEP 11. GLUE IN A STOP.

Once the drawer fits, glue a small strip of wood inside the carcase behind it to serve as a stop. Fully closed, the front of the drawer should be flush with the front of the carcase.

BUILDING THE DOOR

The cabinet door is a typical example of frame-and-panel construction. Traditionally, the panel grooves would have extended all the way through the stiles, and the tenons would have been haunched to fill them. I find it easier, and just as satisfactory, to make simple mortise-and-tenon joints like those in Project 2 and then stop-rout the panel grooves.

The steps for building the cabinet door are as follows:

1. MAKE A CUTTING LIST.

2. SELECT AND MILL THE LUMBER.

3. CUT THE JOINERY.

4. CUT THE PANEL GROOVES.

5. SAW OFF THE STILE ENDS.

6. CUT AND FIT THE PANEL.

7. ASSEMBLE THE DOOR.

8. CLEAN UP THE DOOR.

STEP 1.   MAKE A CUTTING LIST.

Although the cabinet door will end up flush with the sides of the carcase, you should make it about ¹⁄₁₆ in. oversize in order to allow leeway for mistakes, such as the carcase being slightly out of square. The door can be planed to an exact fit after the hinges are mounted, Also, leave the stiles long until the joints are cut and fit. This is another way to minimize the likelihood of error.

Measurements for the door should be taken against the actual size of the carcase. If the door measurements were exactly true to the bottom drawing on p. 164, the cutting list would read as shown at right.

STEP 2.   SELECT AND MILL THE LUMBER.

The grain pattern of the rails and stiles can give a door frame aesthetic appeal. On the other hand, carelessly selected grain can detract from the door's appearance. The drawing below shows two different grain configurations for a door frame. I find the balanced arrangement more attractive because the grain pattern of the rails and stiles relates to the enclosed space within. The grain of the other frame is random by comparison.

The door panel will be the most visually prominent feature of the cabinet, so pick a particularly attractive piece of wood for it. Consider bookmatching if two pieces of wood are required to make up the width (see p. 167).

After the door components have been milled, mark their fronts so all the joinery can be laid out and cut from the same face.

CUTTING LIST FOR DOOR
• 2 pieces at ¾ in. x 1¾ in. x 9⁵⁄₁₆ in. (the rails)
• 2 pieces at ¾ in. x 1½ in. x 18¹⁄₆ in. (the stiles)
• 1 piece at ⅜ in. x 8⁹⁄₁₆ in. x 15¹⁄₁₆ in. (the panel)

GRAIN PATTERN ON A DOOR FRAME

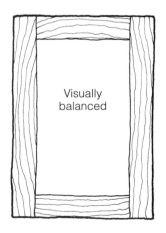

Visually balanced

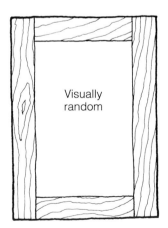

Visually random

MORTISE-AND-TENON PROPORTIONS FOR CABINET DOOR

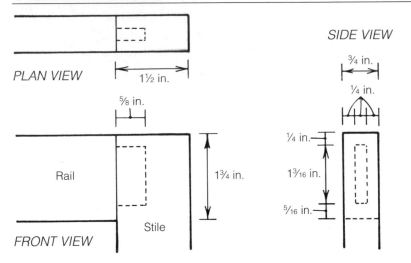

PLAN VIEW

1½ in.

SIDE VIEW

¾ in.

¼ in.

⅝ in.

Rail

Stile

FRONT VIEW

1¾ in.

¼ in.

1³⁄₁₆ in.

⁵⁄₁₆ in.

TENON FOR FRAME-AND-PANEL DOOR

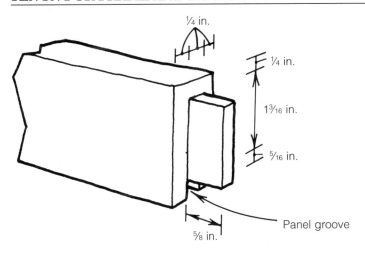

¼ in.

¼ in.

1³⁄₁₆ in.

⁵⁄₁₆ in.

⅝ in.

Panel groove

STEP 3. CUT THE JOINERY.

Join the frame together with simple mortise-and-tenon joinery. Following the rule that the thickness of the mortise should be one-third the thickness of the ¾-in. host piece and that the length of the tenon should be at least twice its thickness, I made my tenons ¼ in. thick and ⅝ in. long. The mortise should be at least ¼ in. from the end of the stile to minimize the chance of the end splitting out during cutting and assembly. The width of the mortise is limited by its intersection with the panel groove. Beyond that point, the groove would eliminate the tenon (see the drawing above).

Transfer the mortise locations from one door stile to the other.

Begin by laying out the mortises on one stile. First, mark the desired overall length of the stile. Leave any extra wood at each end to be trimmed off later. Next, measure in from each end to locate the mortises. When the mortise locations have been laid out on one stile, transfer the marks to the other stile, and scribe the mortise thicknesses with a mortising gauge. Once they are marked, you can cut the mortises by hand (as we did in the earlier projects) or you can try cutting them with a plunge router, as explained in the sidebar on pp. 186-187.

The tenons, like the mortises, are first marked on one rail. Begin by laying out the shoulders so that the distance between them, plus the combined widths of the stiles, adds up to the intended width of the door. Next, mark the tenon lengths, measuring out from the shoulders. Transfer the marks to the other rail. Cut the ends of the rails square at the ends of the tenons. Scribe tenon thickness with the mortising gauge, and mark the tenon widths to match the mortises. (If the mortises were cut with a router, make sure the gauge is set to match an actual mortise.) Finally, cut and fit the tenons, as explained on pp. 110-115.

STEP 4. CUT THE PANEL GROOVES.

The scale drawing calls for grooves $\frac{1}{4}$ in. wide by $\frac{5}{16}$ in. deep. Rout through grooves in the rails and stopped grooves in the stiles. The stopped grooves should extend about $\frac{3}{8}$ in. beyond the inside corners of the frame to accommodate the panel.

MORTISING WITH A PLUNGE ROUTER

One alternative to hand-cutting mortises is to use a plunge router and a simple mortising box. A plunge router is designed so the motor can be moved up and down through the base while running, effectively raising and lowering the cutter. Adjustable stops determine the depth of penetration.

MORTISING BOX

¾ in.

5 in.

1½ in.

5 in.

20 in.

The dimensions given are those of the mortising box shown in the photos.

The mortising box must be deep and wide enough to hold the workpiece and narrow enough that the router base can span the top.

Clamp the workpiece to the inside of the mortising box with its top edge just below the lip.

1. Install a straight or spiral cutter in the router, of the same diameter as the mortise (¼ in. in the case of our cabinet door). Straight bits work well, but spiral cutters chatter less and remove chips more quickly.
2. Mark the mortise on the work.
3. Support the board on a piece of scrap and clamp it to the inside of the mortising box, with the edge to be mortised just below the lip (as shown in the photo above). For routing repeat mortises, as we are doing here, nail stops across the top of the box to keep the travel of the router bit within the confines of the mortise. If you mark the location of the first mortise on the inside of the box and set up the subsequent mortises in exactly the same place, the stops will work for all of them.
4. The router's edge guide will run against the outside of the box, keeping the cutter parallel to the edge of the work. Adjust the guide so the cutter is positioned over the mortise location.
5. With the machine off, lower the cutter until it just touches the

With the edge guide against the outside of the box, rout the mortise in a series of passes, lowering the bit ⅛ in. at each pass.

The rounded ends of the router-cut mortise can be chiseled square, or the tenons can be filed round to fit.

surface of the wood. Set the depth stop to the desired length of travel beyond that point into the wood. Then raise the bit back through the base.

6. Make sure the box is firmly held in place. Then turn the router on and place the edge guide against the side of the box. To avoid burning the cutter or straining the motor, lower the bit

into the mortise about ⅛ in., use the lock lever to hold it there, and move the bit from one end of the mortise to the other. Then lower the bit another ⅛ in. and repeat, until full depth is reached. When the cut is complete, raise the bit back through the base.

An alternative method using the same setup is to make a series of plunge cuts to the full depth of

the mortise, as if you were drilling a series of contiguous holes. After the final plunge cut, sweep the bit through the mortise at full extension to take out the remaining waste.

7. I usually square the rounded ends of router-cut mortises with a chisel, but you could just as well fit the tenons by rounding them with a file.

The cabinet door, glued and clamped.

The cabinet door, disassembled, with all joints and grooves cut.

STEP 5.   SAW OFF THE STILE ENDS.

Dry-assemble the frame and mark the ends of the stiles where they are flush with the outside of the rails. Now disassemble the frame to square the marks around, and saw off the excess.

STEP 6.   CUT AND FIT THE PANEL.

The door panel is the same thickness as the back panel. Giving both panels the same edge treatment enhances the aesthetic coherence of the cabinet (see pp. 174-175 for directions on thinning the panel edges). After fitting the panel to the frame, scrape and sand the panel.

It is easier to prepare the panel and the inside edges of the frame for finishing now, rather than after assembly. Some furniture makers apply finish to the panel at this point, but I prefer to do all the finishing at one time, when the cabinet is fully assembled.

STEP 7.   ASSEMBLE THE DOOR.

Dry-clamp and then glue the door together. Don't apply any glue to the panel or the groove—the panel should remain free to move with changes in humidity.

STEP 8.   CLEAN UP THE DOOR.

After the glue has dried overnight, use a bench or block plane to plane the faces of the door frame flush where the stiles and rails intersect, if they aren't already.

COMPLETING THE CABINET

Once the door has been built, the cabinet is well on its way to completion. The remaining steps are as follows:

1. INSTALL THE DOOR HINGE.

2. MAKE A DOOR PULL.

3. INSTALL A DOOR CATCH.

4. MAKE THE ADJUSTABLE SHELVES.

5. PREPARE THE CABINET FOR HANGING.

6. SCRAPE, SAND AND FINISH THE CABINET.

STEP 1. **INSTALL THE DOOR HINGE.**

A glance through any hardware catalog reveals a variety of hinges. This cabinet design calls for the traditional favorite, brass butt hinges.

Butt hinges vary in quality. Some are pure brass, others are plated; some are well machined, with tight pins, others have loose pins and sloppier movements. The leaves of some are quite thin; others are thick and sturdy. Generally, the best hinges are available at woodworkers' specialty stores and through catalogs, rather than at your local hardware store.

Select hinges that are sized appropriately to the scale of the cabinet. Butt-hinge measurements are given as length by open width. The hinges should not be so wide that their leaves extend into the cabinet interior. Since the sides of the cabinet are ⅝ in. thick, the open width of the hinges should be no more than 1⅜ in. With the pin extending beyond the exterior of the cabinet as it should, such a hinge would cover the full thickness of the cabinet side. Because the hinges I chose for this cabinet measure 1½ in. by 1¼ in., the hinge mortise will only partially span the thickness of the cabinet side.

CABINET HINGES

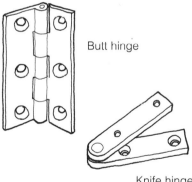

Butt hinge

Knife hinge

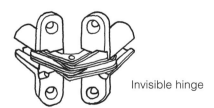

Invisible hinge

Use a marking gauge to scribe the distance the hinge is inset on the carcase.

The hinge mortise can be cut with a router or a chisel.

Before mounting the hinges, choose the side on which the door will open.

To mount hinges:

1. With a pencil, mark the location of the hinges on the carcase at whatever distance from the top and bottom seems pleasing.
2. If you have a narrow hinge that won't cover the full thickness of the cabinet side, set a marking gauge to a hair under the distance from the outside of a hinge leaf to the center of the hinge pin. Use the gauge to scribe the distance each hinge is inset from the outside of the cabinet.
3. Mark the exact ends of the hinge mortises with knife lines squared across the carcase.
4. Pare back to the knife lines from the waste side.
5. Make the hinge mortises a hair deeper than the hinge leaf is thick. Waste can be removed with a router or a chisel. If you use a chisel, scribe the depth of the mortise with a marking gauge to give you a line to work to. If you use a router, set the depth of the cutter to a little more than the thickness of a hinge leaf. A fairly small (¼-in. or ⅜-in. diameter) straight bit lets you rout closer into the corners than

The completed hinge mortises in the cabinet door and carcase.

a larger bit would. Use the router freehand, but be careful not to rout all the way up to the boundaries of the mortise; clean out the waste around the edges with a chisel.

6. Lay the door in the closed position on the carcase and transfer the hinge-location marks to it.

7. Repeat steps 2 through 5 to make hinge mortises in the door.

8. Lay a hinge in each mortise, and mark a pilot hole with an awl at the center of every screw hole. Drill holes slightly smaller than the diameter of the screws. Screws that come prepackaged with hinges are often cheaply made, with thread cut all the way to the head. If so, discard them and buy screws that have a solid shank just below the head. Otherwise, the heads break off too easily.

9. Temporarily mount the hinges to the carcase and the door with just one screw per hinge leaf. Hinges usually have to be mounted and removed several times before the work is finished. Repeated screwing tends to widen holes and loosen the grip of screws.

10. With the door mounted, trace the outline of the carcase onto it. Remember, the door was made slightly oversize to begin with.

11. Remove the hinges and hand-plane the door down to the lines traced from the carcase. When rehinged, the door should fit the carcase perfectly.

DOOR-PULL DESIGN

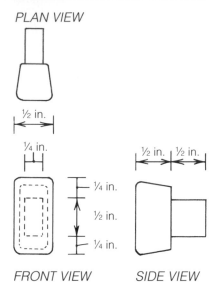

PLAN VIEW

½ in.

¼ in.

¼ in.

½ in.

¼ in.

FRONT VIEW

½ in. ½ in.

SIDE VIEW

The walnut door pull on this cabinet is shaped to echo the dovetail theme.

STEP 2.   MAKE A DOOR PULL.

The design of the door pull deserves thought and attention. It is not only visually important, but is also the part of the cabinet you end up touching the most. It should be pleasing to both the eye and the hand. The drawing above shows the pull I made for my cabinet. It is shaped to echo the dovetail theme, but feel free to design or buy your own pull. Pulls are often made of a contrasting wood—I chose walnut to contrast with the cherry of the cabinet.

Before making the pull, cut the mortise for it in the stile. Next mill a piece of wood to the thickness and width of the pull, but leave it substantially longer to make handling easier while cutting the tenon. When the tenon fits, cut the pull to length. If you are making the pull shown in the drawing above, saw the angled ends with a backsaw. Shape the angled sides with chisels, planes and/or files. Finally, sand the pull and glue it to the door frame.

ENCLOSED-BALL CATCH   KEYHOLE HANGER

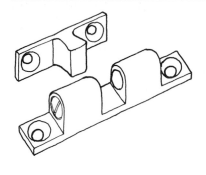 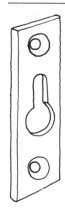

STEP 3.   **INSTALL A DOOR CATCH.**

Hang the door again, one screw per hinge leaf, in order to install
the catch.

Commercially available catches include magnetic, ball and bullet
catches, among others. For a flush-mounted door like the one on my
cabinet, I prefer an enclosed ball catch (see the drawing above left),
though its two halves must be installed to close tolerances.

To install an enclosed ball catch, decide where the catch will be
located and mark a centerline onto the frame and door. Mark the
center of each catch part as well. Mount the parts with centers aligned.
Once the catch is installed, remove it and the hinges in preparation for
sanding and finishing.

STEP 4.   **MAKE THE ADJUSTABLE SHELVES.**

If there are going to be wooden shelves in the cabinet, this is the time
to make them. They should be about 1/16 in. shorter in width and length
than the cabinet interior. They can be as thin as 1/4 in., or thicker if you
like. An alternative is to use glass shelves with polished edges, which
can be ordered from a local glass company.

STEP 5.   **PREPARE THE CABINET FOR HANGING.**

The most straightforward way to hang the cabinet would be to drill a
couple of holes through the mounting piece and screw it to the wall. If
the sight of screw heads inside the cabinet would be unappealing, you
can use commercial hardware that attaches to the back of the
mounting piece. My favorite is a keyhole hanger (see the drawing
above right), which is mortised flush with the back of the cabinet and
has a hole drilled underneath the keyhole to accept a screw head. The
hanger drops over the head of a screw sticking out from the wall. Two
keyhole hangers should be used to keep a cabinet hanging level.

Make whatever holes or mortises are required for the hanging
system you have chosen.

The completed cabinet.

STEP 6. SCRAPE, SAND AND FINISH THE CABINET.

With all hardware removed, scrape and sand all surfaces on the carcase, drawer and door that were not prepared earlier. Use 120- or 150-grit sandpaper. Wet all parts to raise the grain. Let them dry overnight, and then sand with 220-grit paper.

Apply the finish of your choice. Be careful not to let it puddle and dry in the interstices between the panels and frames. (See pp. 156-160 for a more detailed discussion of finishing.)

When the cabinet is fully finished, reinstall the hardware. The cabinet is now complete.

AFTERWORD

This book offers a solid grounding in the basics of woodworking. Having read it, you probably know what you would like to learn next, and wonder how to go about it.

There is a wealth of information available through books, classes and, most important, hands-on trial and error.

Among the informative books on woodworking techniques are many by the publisher of this one, The Taunton Press. Through reading, you will discover that different authors suggest different ways of doing things. Remember, there is no one right way. With experience, you will develop methods of woodworking that are right for you—approaches that enhance your pleasure in the process and yield the results you are looking for.

Instruction is available through community colleges, degree programs, apprenticeships and workshops. A good instructor is invaluable, but not always easy to find. I particularly recommend workshops as a wonderful opportunity. Their intensive nature, along with the extensive interaction with faculty and other students, creates an atmosphere in which a tremendous amount of learning takes place.

In the long run, most learning comes through the experience of your own hands. Practice and observation are the two most reliable instructors in craftsmanship. I encourage you to design projects that extend your range of skills.

Above all, keep sight of the reasons you have chosen to pursue craftsmanship. The finished object is, at best, a reflection of the true rewards of the process—the personal sense of quality, joy and integrity that comes from work well done.

SOURCES OF SUPPLY

The following companies sell woodworking tools through mail order. Most of them offer a catalog; inquire individually as to availability and cost.

Bridge City Tool Works
1104 N. E. 28th Avenue
Portland, OR 97232
(800) 253-3332

Albert Constantine & Son
2050 Eastchester Road
Bronx, NY 10461
(212) 792-1600

Garrett Wade Company
161 Avenue of the Americas
New York, NY 10013
(800) 221-2942

Highland Hardware
1045 N. Highland Avenue
Atlanta, GA 30306
(404) 872-4466

Robert Larson Company, Inc.
33 Dorman Avenue
San Francisco, CA 94124
(800) 356-2195

Lee Valley Tools, Ltd.
1080 Morrison Drive
Ottawa, Ontario
Canada K2H 8K7
(800) 267-8767

Leichtung Tools
4944 Commerce Parkway
Cleveland, OH 44128
(800) 321-6840

Seven Corners Hardware
216 West Seventh Street
St. Paul, MN 55102
(800) 328-0457

Woodcraft Supply Corp.
210 Wood County Industrial Park
Parkersburg, WV 26102-1686
(800) 542-9115

Woodline/The Japan Woodworker
1731 Clement Avenue
Alameda, CA 94501
(800) 537-7820

The Woodworkers' Store
21801 Industrial Boulevard
Rogers, MN 55374
(612) 428-3200

Woodworker's Supply of New Mexico
5604 Alameda, N. E.
Albuquerque, NM 87113
(800) 645-9292

INDEX

Editor: *Peter Chapman*
Designer/Layout Artist: *Catherine Cassidy*
Copy/Production Editor: *Ruth Dobsevage*
Photographer, except where noted: *Hal Smyer*

Typeface: *Garamond*
Paper: *Warren Patina Matte, 70 lb., neutral pH*
Printer: *Arcata Graphics/Hawkins, New Canton, Tennessee*